Sensitive Midwifery

SENSITIVE MIDWIFERY

Caroline Flint SRN SCM

Illustrations by Helen Chown BA(Hons) Fine Art

Heinemann Nursing

Heinemann Nursing
An imprint of Heinemann Professional Publishing Ltd
Halley Court, Jordan Hill, Oxford OX2 8EJ

OXFORD   LONDON   SINGAPORE
NAIROBI   IBADAN   KINGSTON

First published 1986
Reprinted 1986, 1987, 1989, 1990

ISBN 0 433 10620 4

Typeset by Wilmaset, Birkenhead
and printed and bound in Great Britain by
Biddles Ltd, Guildford and King's Lynn

Contents

Preface

It may sound presumptuous to write a book entitled *Sensitive Midwifery* as if I somehow had a prerogative in sensitivity. Nevertheless I feel that the title should stand as few of the ideas are actually mine. Instead the book is a collection of many of the ideas and thoughts that I have been taught by others — by midwives, mothers, doctors, my friends in the National Childbirth Trust, my sisters in the Association of Radical Midwives, my colleagues in the Royal College of Midwives, my own mother, the midwife who delivered my first baby and many, many other very sensitive people who have influenced my thinking, my ideas and the way I tick.

I have few original ideas of my own. My talent is that I listen and absorb what I hear. In my head I keep all the ideas I have ever heard or seen. I gestate them and they pop up at times when I need them. Thus the book *Sensitive Midwifery* is a collection of the ideas and thoughts of many people who are sensitive to the needs of pregnant and labouring women. Very few of the ideas are mine and, if you see an idea here that seems familiar, it is probably yours, and I'm sorry if your name isn't acknowledged but perhaps you can gain comfort from the fact that you are obviously influencing people's thoughts in a practical way.

Especially to the following people must I acknowledge their influence on my thinking — Miss Waldie, Margaret Arnold, Sheila Kitzinger, Hazel Smith, Nicky Lean, Dr Leslie Rutty, Michel Odent, Mrs Harrop, Sally Inch, Chloe Fisher, Jane Farebrother, Mary Cronk, Marianne Scruggs, Gwen Rankin, Joan Gibson, Dora Henschell and the person who for two and a half lovely years encouraged me to put yours and my ideas into practice, Lynette Murray.

This book has been harder to write than I anticipated but yet more pleasure than I expected. The fact that it has actually finally emerged is due to the encouragement and help of Giles Flint, Cathy Watson of Heinemann and Helen Chown. For expert help and criticism, I wish to give grateful thanks to Ann

Stewart, Joan Greenwood, Marion Lee, Phillipa Gunn, Regeina Hastings, Mavis Manderson and Lolita Sykes.

To be a midwife is to be with women (the meaning of the Anglo Saxon word) — sharing their travail and their suffering, their joys and their delights. To be a midwife is to engage in a close and intimate relationship which often lasts only as long as the pregnancy, birth and puerperium but the effect of which travels down through the centuries in the image women have of themselves and their abilities and worth.

Midwives and women are intertwined, whatever affects women affects midwives and vice versa — we are interrelated and interwoven. When midwives are strong, women are able to labour safely and without interference. When midwives are weak, women's bodies are taken over and the birth process is interfered with often to the detriment of women.

For us to practise as true midwives, for us to learn to be close to women and to have empathy with them, we must first get to know and love the woman who is nearest to us — ourselves.

Chapter One

Introduction

Mothers and midwives are intertwined like Siamese twins —
whatever happens to midwives affects women and whatever
happens to women affects midwives. Midwives need to be
strong and loving and sensitive to the needs of women; only
then can women feel secure in the momentous experiences that
surround the birth of a child.

A woman never forgets her midwife. Years after the actual
event she will be able to remember with clarity what the
midwife said, what the midwife did, how the midwife reacted.

How the midwife treats the woman can affect the woman's
perception of herself, her feelings about herself as a mother, her
concept of herself as a woman. The midwife also affects the
man — she can help him feel strong and competent in his new
role as a father, or she can make him feel a nuisance and in the
way. The midwife sets the scene for the emergence of a new
family — she is the cornerstone of the emotional health of our
whole community.

For midwives to be able to love, cherish and care for women
throughout pregnancy, labour and the puerperium, midwives
need to be loved, cherished and cared for themselves. We work
in an emotional minefield. Every word, every expression on
our faces, every comment, perhaps even our very thoughts are
remembered for ever by the women we look after. Our effect
on society is far reaching and permanent. We are never
forgotten.

To work as a midwife is stressful, because to work effectively
and sensitively, the midwife gives so much of herself, and she
becomes so involved with and such a part of the family with
which she is involved. To enable her to be a fount of such
strength, a source of so much comfort, she herself must have
support and cherishing.

A midwife who wants to care for women beautifully needs
first of all to set up a support system for herself. If she is lucky,
she may already have a supportive and cherishing partner/lover/
sister/parent/husband, but frequently these delightful alterna-

tives are not around and the midwife has to consciously set about forming a support network for herself.

Over the years nurses and frequently midwives have been exhorted 'don't get involved', and a criticism of nurses and midwives has been to say 'she gets too involved with her patients'. But it becomes increasingly obvious that many people become nurses and midwives *because* they want to become emotionally involved in other people's lives. Furthermore, the one overriding quality that most women want of their attendants during pregnancy, labour and the puerperium is that they be emotionally involved with them — interested in them as people and not just as slabs of pregnant human flesh to be 'treated'.

SUPPORT NETWORKS

If you are lucky, you already have a supportive family network, or perhaps you belong to a supportive and caring church. You may be lucky and have loving friends. But the most important people to cherish you in your role as a midwife are other people who are as interested in and concerned about midwifery and childbirth as you are yourself. This could be a group of the Association of Radical Midwives, it could be members of the National Childbirth Trust or it could be members of the Association for Improvements in the Maternity Service or one of the other consumer groups. But if these groups do not immediately appeal to you, there is a group that you already know, a group who would be overjoyed to cherish and care for you, a group who would be thrilled to hear from you — and that is the group of parents whose babies you have delivered, or who you have looked after antenatally or postnatally, or who have been participants in your antenatal classes. They already care about you and remember you and would be overjoyed to hear from you.

So how do you go about it? First, it is a good idea from the moment you start your training to have a register of all the women you have delivered. Registers are available from Hymns Ancient and Modern Ltd at a cost of £1.95 each (see Appendix 4 for address). A hardbacked exercise book, however, would probably be just as effective.

Then it is worth sending 'your babies' a birthday card, or

writing to each mother and asking her how the baby is and saying how much you would like to see them all again. It would be a good idea to start by asking the woman how you could have made things better for her during her labour/pregnancy or puerperium and by being open to her suggestions. By doing this with more and more women, you will become aware of how important you were to them. It will show you how important everything you do or say is to everyone you are with during this very sensitive time. Also you will become aware of the deep feeling of love that these people have towards you, and how deeply you yourself feel towards them. Together you have been through an experience which has changed their lives. It will also have changed yours, although you might not have noticed at the time.

Build up a group of women with whom you can go and have coffee when you are off duty, for whom you can babysit and run to the shops, and who can do the odd bit of shopping for you. It is important for you to live closely with young families who love you. It is also important for you to have somewhere where you can talk about your work and about what is happening to you. You need someone to confide in who listens from a position of love and concern for you, and you need someone who is as fascinated by childbirth and midwifery and everything that surrounds it as you are.

In an ideal world, the support and cherishing we need in order to do our job properly would come from within our own profession and from our own colleagues. At this point in our history, sadly, we often have to go outside our profession for cherishing and love and to find others who are as enthusiastic and fascinated about childbirth and women as we are. Support may not be forthcoming from colleagues because they may not want to 'talk shop' when they are off duty. I suggest that the reason that we often have to go outside our own profession for nurturing is because our profession at this time is emotionally impoverished.

PROBLEMS FACING MIDWIVES

Look around at your colleagues. Although many, of course, will be well-rounded and fulfilled women, there will be many others who are suffering from burdens which are so intolerable that it makes it very hard to have enough love to spare for other people, let alone for other midwives.

Some of your colleagues may be childless, because of infertility problems, because they are single or because they are past childbearing age. Even for midwives who have produced their desired number of beloved children, sometimes pangs of jealousy and envy overwhelm them when looking after a pregnant woman, and sometimes the longing to take a baby home with you is strong. It is very hard for any woman to have to come to terms with childlessness. When she is daily reminded of the fact that she is childless and likely to remain so, it is like a knife turning in a wound. To function fully as a woman delivering other women's babies, the childless midwife needs the opportunity to look at her own feelings and come to terms with them. This is not something we do very often in the nursing, medical or midwifery professions. To come to terms with painful realities, we need hours of talking with non-judgmental, caring friends. How many childless midwives have this opportunity?

To be unable to have children is a great source of grief, and some of the insensitive treatment of parturient women is a result of this unresolved grief within our profession. Some of the unkind treatment of younger midwives may be something to do with this grief and anger from women who will never have children towards those who probably will.

Many of your colleagues will be struggling to survive. They may be the breadwinner in the family. Their partner or husband may be unemployed or they may be single parents. Midwives earn low salaries, and a financial struggle pulls people down. They feel drained, afraid for the future and worried about debts. Often they are below par because they are not eating properly. They feel cold at home because they cannot afford heating. They feel depressed and overwhelmed, and they have no room to help and cherish other women because they are suffering too much themselves.

Some of your colleagues may be experiencing emotional struggles. They have to be the emotional support for the whole family. They may have a partner who is unemployed or who is in a job which is far below his abilities. Instead of feeling bolstered up by their partner, these midwives have constantly to shore up the battered ego of their partner. They frequently have no emotional giving to spare — they need a source of strength themselves.

Many midwives are also mothers. They need to work outside the home and with this comes all the problems of organising babyminders or childcare, and all the accompanying feelings of guilt towards the child. These midwives have to run a job, run a home and organise childcare — which always seems to be precarious. Does everyone's babyminder always break her leg on the first day of the school holidays? These midwives have so much on their plate that they are unable to offer support and cherishing — they often need it too much themselves.

Many midwives have mothering problems. When I talk to midwives I am often surprised at how few of them have managed to breastfeed their babies for any length of time. There are, of course, notable exceptions to this, but it is exceedingly difficult to encourage and support a woman through a breast-feeding crisis if you have trodden the same path yourself and not managed. Equally, a midwife who deeply believes that breastfeeding works and who tries to help a woman through the crisis may be surprised at the strength of feeling against her 'fanaticism' in 'insisting that this woman should continue when the poor soul has such sore nipples/fair skin/lack of milk/

exhaustion/small nipples/big nipples'. The reason that feelings run so high is because midwives are dealing with an emotional minefield. It is not for nothing that the National Childbirth Trust, the La Leche League and the Association of Breastfeeding Mothers insist that their counsellors have successfully breastfed babies for a significant period; these women know deep in their psyche that breastfeeding works and that it is worth striving for.

Many midwives experience problems of race. Many midwives are not English, and they suffer all the problems that racially disadvantaged groups suffer. People discriminate against them. They often feel alienated and feel they have little in common with either their colleagues or the women they are caring for. When promotion comes along they are often not chosen for posts they are more than adequate to fill. They find it hard to develop professionally because it is other midwives who are sent on courses, other midwives who are asked to speak in public, and other midwives who are asked to represent their profession.

It is almost impossible for the person who thinks she is being racially discriminated against to voice this suspicion. It is always denied. Furthermore as it is often unconscious discrimination, the person who is being discriminated against is made to feel that it has nothing to do with her colour or her racial origin and that it is because she is not of sufficient calibre that the incident has happened. This, of course, makes her feel even worse and makes her question her own abilities.

CHERISHING OURSELVES

In order to cherish and support women through their experience of childbirth, we need to feel loved and cherished ourselves. We can start the cherishing process by cherishing ourselves.

Many of us have a punitive streak in us — a remnant perhaps from our nursing training. We find it difficult to go off duty early even though we are owed hours of time. We feel guilty if we are extravagant with the money we have worked hard to earn. We feel we must toil even if there is really no work to be done. We are not good at spoiling ourselves.

You are a good midwife. The very fact that you are reading this book shows that you care about your profession and that you are interested and concerned about your own development as a midwife. Acknowledge how good you are. *Give yourself a prize for being such a good midwife.*

Every time I walk in to the house, my husband chimes out with 'Hello Super Midwife' or 'Here comes Super Midwife'. Constant positive encouraging words like this have to have a positive effect on us. I'm sorry I can't spare him to lend out — he's needed too much here — but remember always to address yourself in a loving way. Never tell yourself that you are a fool or stupid. When you talk to yourself, always call yourself 'Darling' or 'Clever Girl' or 'Super Midwife'. Do this to your colleagues too. If we all call ourselves by loving names, it will have a positive benefit for our profession.

Now, 'Super Midwife', the next way you are going to cherish yourself is to give yourself a treat. Give yourself ten minutes. It is your time. It belongs to you.

Go to your bedroom, take off your shoes and lie on your bed. Make sure all your limbs are supported — perhaps have a pillow under each knee, one under your head and perhaps one under each arm. Make sure every limb is completely supported. Let the pillows which are supporting you take all your weight. Let all expression go from your face — let your jaw hang loosely. Listen to yourself breathing — be aware at each outgoing breath of your relaxation increasing — becoming deeper and deeper. Listen to your breathing . . . listen to your heart beating. Be aware of the miracle of your own beautiful body. Without any conscious effort on your part, your food is being digested, your blood is being circulated, your entire being is being oxygenated. Your body is beautiful and beautifully made — women's bodies are wondrous and they *work* — they ovulate, menstruate, give birth, breathe, walk, run, eat, talk. You are a miraculous being.

Make sure that you are still relaxed. If there are any points of tension in your body, push them down into the bed and then let them go.

Be aware of the warmth which is filling your body, the feeling of lightness and the feeling of being rested, and the sense of well-being.

Now, if you have only read those words, please now go and *do* them. The delights and pleasures of relaxation are enormously beneficial to our sense of well-being. We need to relax as often as we can. It helps us to appreciate our bodies and to love ourselves.

MORE CHERISHING

The best way for me to cherish myself is to have a long, luxurious, deep bath. I find that it strengthens me and I am fit for anything — whether that anything is another day's work or a night's sleep. Some people do not feel like that about baths — they find them sapping — but, for those who do, in order to cherish yourself, there are certain basic essentials that you need when you bathe. The bath must be clean before you use it. The water must be hot. The soap you use must be lovely — smelling gorgeous and of a rich texture. The towel you dry yourself with must be clean, dry and fluffy. After your bath, the lotion or talc you use needs to smell lovely.

I am being serious about the smells. For you to love yourself, your smell needs to fascinate you. If you have been given some scents as a present and you do not like them, it is not helpful to you to use them. You are not a dustbin — you are a very special midwife and you should use only the best as far as you can.

Because you are such a special person, you need to make sure that all the fabrics that touch your body feel lovely — your knickers should feel soft and silky, your bra should be comfortable, and you should use very soft and comfortable lavatory paper. It is important to become more and more aware of your own body. This helps you to feel cherished and loved but it also helps you to appreciate what is happening inside the women you are looking after, and it helps you to appreciate their bodies more.

The next stage in your cherishing of yourself is to write a list of all the things you are good at:

Name
The things I am very good at are
1
2
3
4
5

6
7
8
9
10
11
12
13
14
15

The things I am just good at are
1
2
3
4
5

No thank you, I do not want to know the things you are bad at or even mediocre at. You are such a special person that I know you will be able to fill in all 20 spaces with just a little thought. So please start now and fill them in, and then go on to fill in the next list.

Name
The things that give me great pleasure are
1
2
3
4
5
6
7
8
9
10
11
12
13
14
15

The things which I dislike are
1
2
3
4
5

Now that you have identified what pleases you, it is worth trying to make sure that you experience some of these pleasures every week. Each reader will have a different list. My list of pleasures would include:

- Listening to Mozart
- Having a bath
- Eating certain chocolates
- Lying completely relaxed
- Cuddling
- Watching a baby's head crowning
- Watching someone else working
- Going to the theatre
- Watching trees
- Squeezing bottoms
- Receiving presents
- Having my hair cut

Other ways of cherishing your body are not difficult. If you are feeling stiff or even just tired, massage can be very comforting. It is lovely if done by someone else, but very satisfactory if you do it.

Start with a lotion that smells lovely to you.
Put some on your hands and start by massaging your feet and legs — finding out what feels nice.
Put more lotion on your hands and then massage your abdomen in circular movements, then massage up to your ribs and your breasts.
Put more lotion on your hands and then massage your shoulders one at a time, massaging them for a long time, rotating really deeply. Now massage your neck with both hands, be aware of the heaviness of your head and of the relationship between head and neck. Now massage your face, around your eyes, circular motions on your cheeks, deep circular movements at your temples, then straight across your forehead.

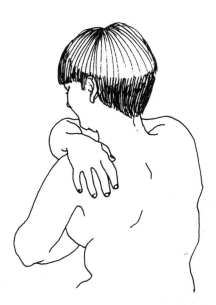

Be aware of how refreshed your face feels now. Be aware of how your whole body feels — refreshed, invigorated, alive.

Get to know your body, cherish it and love it, learn about how it feels, massage and pamper it. You need to love and respect your body in order to cherish other women's bodies during childbirth.

EVEN MORE CHERISHING

We all need a 'lovely box'. This is either a box or a file which contains all the lovely appreciative letters you have been sent, photos of magic times or of beloved friends, and mementos of special occasions. This box is for times when you feel rather unloved and alone. You go and look through your 'lovely box' and it shows you how special you really are and how many people really appreciate you.

Together with your lovely box (if that name is driving you mad, try 'memory lane' or 'memento box' or 'instant pick-up' instead), you need an exercise book. In this you write down details of all the very special moments you have experienced —

those times of heightened sensitivity which remain clear and bright in your memory.

The patron saint of midwives probably gives us more insight into the personality of the midwife than anything else. Look at your badge, or look at the badge on the community midwife's hat, and there you will see the patron saint of midwives — a Roman pagan goddess, Juno Lucina, goddess of sensuality and sexuality. Here is the root of the mystery, the magic and the sensitivity of the midwife, her history as the wise woman, the witch burned at the stake, the healer, the helper and comforter of labouring women, a history that reaches back into the mists of time, the oldest profession of all.

To be a midwife is to be with women (the meaning of the Anglo Saxon word), sharing their travail and their suffering, their joys and their delights. To be a midwife is to engage in a close and intimate relationship which often lasts only as long as the pregnancy, birth and puerperium but the effect of which travels down through the centuries in the image women have of themselves and their abilities and worth.

Midwives and women are intertwined, whatever affects women affects midwives and vice versa — we are interrelated and interwoven. When midwives are strong, women can labour safely and without interference. When midwives are weak, women's bodies are taken over and the birth process is interfered with, often to the detriment of women.

For us to practise as true midwives, for us to learn to be close to women and to have empathy with them, we must first get to know and love the woman who is nearest to us — ourselves.

Chapter Two

Pregnancy

What choices do women really have? Can a woman really decide where to have her baby, how to have her baby, what sort of antenatal care and what sort of postnatal care to have? I wish I could put my hand on my heart and say 'Yes, of course, women have a choice'. But if I am to be truthful, I have to say that I believe that women have very little choice if they are intelligent and articulate, and that they have even less if they are inarticulate. I also have to say that I believe that it is only by you and I opening up choices to women that they will ever have any.

Why do I think that it is important for women to have choices? Does it really matter? Can't we just get on and decide what is best for these women and tell them? At least we would be secure in the knowledge that we had given the advice we thought was the best, at least we would be comfortable — or would we?

Before we begin, let us look at the nature of motherhood. What is a mother? Some of us are mothers and our feelings about mothers will be coloured by what we see as the essentials for mothering our own children. (For me when my children were smallish, the essential was for them to have polished shoes. If my children's shoes were gleaming, I felt like a 'good mother', despite the fact that we might have run out of loo paper and baked beans. If their shoes were dirty, on the other hand, no matter how full the cupboards, how nutritious the meals, how enjoyable the games — I felt like a 'bad mother'.)

To explore the nature of motherhood, I suggest that we need to think back as far as we can to our own mothers and our memories of them, that we try to recapture the feelings of being a little child again, try to remember what it was like.

I can remember vividly the smell of my mother when I was a very little girl. I can also remember sitting in my pram and her talking to me. I can remember her and Dad making my bed after I had wet it in the night. Even now when I have had a bath, it makes me recall very vividly the lovely feeling of talcum between my toes and the lovely cuddly feeling of being dried on my mother's lap. I can remember sitting on a bus and feeling scornful of the other children on the bus because all their mothers were so plain and ugly and mine was so beautiful.

The amazing thing about my mother was that she was not only beautiful, but she knew *everything* — not only what food was nutritious and therefore must be eaten, but also who was going to win the war, what time little girls should be in bed by, what little girls should and should not do, whether the little Princesses had a bedtime story, whether worms minded when Grandpa's spade sliced them in two, even whether worms went to heaven. She was *brilliant* — she was also my whole world, and unfortunately she was also the whole world of both my smaller sisters so I had to bite and punch them frequently to keep them in their place.

I am sure my experience of my mother will tally with yours in many respects. I am sure your perception of your mother when you were little was that she was beautiful (the beloved is always perceived as beautiful) and that she knew everything. We probably had the same sort of experience when we were in our teens and discovered that in actual fact our mothers *knew nothing.*

This all-knowing and beautiful deity is probably a common perception of the mother by her offspring and this is the role we are helping the woman to take on when she is expecting her baby. She is the source of all for this little child — all knowledge, all nutrition, all power — and it seems to me that to try to prepare her for this by alienating her from herself and her roots by taking away her clothes, by infantilising her, by removing her pubic hair, by destroying her spirit by conducting intimate examinations in secret and private parts of her body, and perhaps above all by telling her what is good for her without giving her the opportunity to decide for herself is perhaps the most crazy way imaginable to prepare women for the most dynamic and influential role of their lives.

Our role as midwives is to help a woman grow in confidence during her pregnancy. We are in a unique position to do this because we are geared to the normality of pregnancy and labour, and we expect in our heart of hearts that everything will come out right. (Not for us is the damaging assumption that 'everything is normal only in retrospect' which, as *The Role of the Midwife* so rightly points out, is the philosophy which has harmed our professional independence more than any other single factor in recent years.)

How do we help the woman to grow in confidence during her pregnancy? How do we help her to mature from a single carefree person — who, although she may be tied by bonds of affection to others, is basically free — to someone who will be tied forever to another human being? How do we help her to take on this enormously heavy burden in such a way as to enable her to carry it comfortably? How do we help her to grow from a girl into a woman?

HELPING A WOMAN TO BE CONFIDENT

Perhaps the most important way to increase someone's confidence is to listen to them and to show respect towards them, what they have to say, their culture, their ideas and their customs. Here I am not just talking about ideas and customs which are different because the woman comes from another country. We all have different backgrounds — different influences have shaped us. If we are brought up in Godalming, our ideas about how women behave will be different from those of people brought up in Glasgow. If we are brought up to see food as an 'occasion' (because we always sit round a table set with knives and forks and talk while we eat), we will feel differently about food than if we are used to eating our food standing up in the kitchen, or off a tray in front of the telly. Our upbringings give us different expectations and needs.

Having suggested that we should encourage women to talk to us and that we should then listen with respect to what they say, it then behoves us to think about the circumstances in which we are trying to encourage them to talk. Have you ever been a 'patient'? Can you recall going to the family planning clinic or to a gynae out-patients clinic?

When you went in, you were not sure where to go. Did anyone help you? When you had waited for a long time and were getting upset because you wondered if anyone knew you were there, did you do anything about it? Did you go and find a nurse and demand to know why you were being kept waiting for so long? Or did you just sit there being 'good' because you did not want to trouble the nurses?

When you went in to see the doctor, what were you dressed in? Were you in your own clothes or someone else's gown? When the doctor or nurse looked at you, could they see what sort of person you are? Could they see that you are a caring, compassionate professional woman who reads books to enhance your knowledge in your spare time?

When you talked to the doctor could you speak freely and in a relaxed way? Did you feel that he or she had hours of time to spend just with you? Or did you gabble so that you could get all the vital information across in just a few minutes because you knew that he or she was a busy person and you didn't want to 'waste their time'? Are you really that unimportant? For whose benefit was that clinic running? Who were the most important people there?

If a midwife who works in the health service and who works and is friends with doctors and nurses can feel intimidated and disoriented by a visit to a clinic, what must it do to women who have never been to a hospital before, except perhaps to see their grandpa when he was dying? Hospitals are frightening — there really are people who faint on hospital doorsteps because of the smell of hospitals.

So we have a woman who has no experience of hospital except for the death of someone, who has no experience of what to expect, who has been told by friends that she will be 'examined'. She comes to an alien place and first of all she cannot find where she is supposed to go. 'Antenatal' to you and me means pregnancy — to how many other people does it mean that?

Having finally found that 'Antenatal' means pregnancy, the woman, who until this moment has felt special and unique, experiencing a new and delicious secret happening inside her body, comes into the antenatal clinic and sees before her a vast sea of pregnant women. What does this do to her confidence? Is she unique and special? Or are we saying to her 'you are unimportant, just merely one of hundreds'?

She arrives hot and breathless because her appointment letter says 2 p.m. and she had problems locating the clinic. She looks at her watch and sees that it is five minutes past two and says to the receptionist — 'I'm sorry I'm late'. The receptionist smiles at her and tells her where to sit. She sits and sits, wondering if she had better remind the receptionist that she is here because they seem to have forgotten her. She is dying to urinate but she dare not go because now and then nurses (are they nurses?) come out of doors and call out names and she might miss hers. There is a frightful noise in the clinic and it is very difficult to hear what names the nurses are actually calling.

Finally her name is called, the nurse says 'Follow me' and then charges off at a rate of knots. The woman, who by now is nearly wetting herself, hobbles along behind her. The nurse takes her into a tiny room (a cupboard really) and says 'everything off and put this on'. This can be a dressing gown (it smells of sweat, someone else has been wearing it) or a gown (it does not tie up, my bottom is showing). She sits in the cupboard, now nearly weeping with fear and a full bladder. Finally the nurse pops her head round the door and says in a friendly voice, 'Hello, I'm Staff Midwife Richards. Come and sit in here because I want to ask you a few questions'.

What do we have to do to make it better than that?

The ideal is probably to conduct the initial interview with the woman in her own home, so that the midwife is the visitor and the woman and her partner are in their own surroundings.

If this is out of the question and the woman has to come to the antenatal clinic, how can we make it easier and more pleasant for her? How can we make it an experience in which she grows in confidence rather than one in which she feels humiliated?

Think about how you would welcome an honoured guest into your own home. Before she came, you would write to her and welcome her and you would make clear what she was coming to, i.e. an invitation to dinner at 7.30 for 8, or coffee at 11 a.m. You would not expect the honoured guest to just turn up at any time and to stay for hours. Both she and you need to know when you expect her to come and how long you expect her to be there. This is the very least we should be doing for our honoured guests — the women who are coming to book in our unit.

Here is a sample letter inviting a woman to an antenatal clinic.

St Nib's Hospital

Dear Mrs Smith,
Welcome to St Nib's Hospital. We hope you will be happy with your visits to us and we hope we shall be able to help you to have a happy and healthy pregnancy.

Your first appointment with us is in the antenatal clinic (that's on the ground floor of the block just inside the Readley Road entrance — the 63 and 49 bus stop outside the gate) on Monday July 6 at 2 p.m.

When you come, please go and say hello to the lady at the desk just inside the front door. She is called Barbara and it is her job to look after women who are coming for the first time. She will give you a small bottle and will show you where the lavatory is because we would like a specimen of urine from you, please.

The next thing that will happen will be . . . and so on

Your visit will probably take two hours, so bring a book or magazine to read so that you don't get too fed-up with waiting.

With best wishes,
Midwife Jones

Now she is prepared for what is likely to happen to her, the woman will feel less intimidated. We have also made clear that we are at her service and that the service we are running is for her.

I work in a team of midwives called the Know Your Midwife Team. When we write and invite women to join our scheme, we send them a photo of the four of us. Under the photo are details

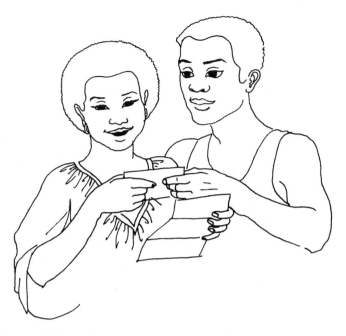

about us so that the women can get to know who they will see before they arrive. Women have been most appreciative of this — they say that it helps a lot to know something about the people you are going to meet.

So we have sent a welcoming letter to the woman explaining what her visit will consist of and how long she will be at the clinic. We have also let her know who she will be meeting.

When an honoured guest actually arrives at our house, what is the first thing we usually do? We take her coat and hang it up somewhere safe, and we offer her a cup of tea or coffee. So we are sitting comfortably, midwife and pregnant woman, both with our clothes on, sipping a cup of tea together. How do we get her to talk to us and how do we help to increase her self-confidence?

I usually start by saying who I am. 'Hello, I'm Caroline. I'm a midwifery sister and I've worked here for four years. I've got three children who are all teenagers now, and my husband is called Giles. We live near Crystal Palace.' Usually the woman then follows suit and tells me what her name is and a few quick details about herself. Then I show her the notes I am going to be filling in, and I ask her if that is all right and if she is comfortable or needs to go to the lavatory first or anything.

Most midwives are fairly circumscribed by the medical notes

Photocredit: Mark Ellidge

PENNY CHURCH

I am 30 years old. My interests are music, sport and reading. I trained as a general nurse at the Westminster Hospital. I trained as a Midwife at St. George's Hospital and the South London Hospital. I am very actively involved in my local church, and like the other three midwives in the team, I enjoy being with pregnant women and I enjoy delivering babies.

CLAIRE NEILL

I am married and I have two children, called Anne Marie who is 13, and Vaughan who is 10. I am interested in music, reading and going to the theatre. I did my general training at the Whittington Hospital, and I trained as a midwife at Rochford. I very much enjoy being a midwife and delivering babies.

CAROLINE FLINT

I live near Crystal Palace with my husband Giles, and our three children, Matt 18, Rebecca (Bo) 16, and Tom who is 14. My interests are writing, listening to Mozart, walking in the country, going to the theatre and talking. I love being a midwife and delivering babies, and have been looking forward to this scheme starting for some years.

WENDY PEARCE

I am 28 and I am interested in music, photography and running, in fact any sport really. I am divorced and have one daughter who is called Nancy and is 4. I trained as a general nurse at Guy's Hospital, and I trained as a midwife at St. George's and the South London Hospital. Another of my interests, of course, is childbirth and being a midwife.

we have to fill in. Keep an eye on these and realise that you will almost always be filling them in in the same order as the questions appear and that this may not be the best order in which to ask them. In order for the woman to tell us about what is important for her, we need to ask some open-ended questions and we need to sit quietly, waiting for her to answer.

What would you like us to call you? Names are so important, and it is so much more comfortable to be called by your own name than by another name — even if your own name is not the name on your birth certificate.

Have you any brothers and sisters? How were you all born? Here we have a chance to find out what this woman's conditioning to childbirth has been, how her mother had her children and how this woman feels about birth.

How were you all fed? Here we have a chance to discuss breast and bottle feeding with the woman, helping her to begin to think about how she is going to feed her baby.

How did you feel when you first realised you were pregnant? A time for her to vocalise the doubts and fears as well as the pleasure she might have had at the beginning of her pregnancy.

What about now? How are you feeling now?

And your partner, how has he reacted? A question to be asked of the man if he is there, of course.

What about where you live — is it all right to take a baby back there?

After the baby is born, you'll need someone to help you with the washing, shopping and cooking for a week or two. Have you any ideas at the moment about who could help? This will help the woman to think about life after the baby and what it might be like.

Do your family live near you? Will they be able to help you at all when you come out of hospital?

What about your job? Will you be going back to work after the baby is born? How do you feel about that?

What about hospital? How do you feel about coming in to hospital? Have you ever been in hospital before?

Have you ever had anything to do with babies and young children before? A chance for us to suggest a visit to the postnatal ward to see some new babies and mothers.

What about when you have the baby? Is there anything special you would like when your baby is being born? This is probably the most important question of all. Most women will say that they have not thought about it much yet. Others will say that they will leave it to us, the experts. But for the woman who has already thought a great deal about her plans for labour and who has very definite priorities, being able to tell us about them is an enormous relief. The fact that we have initiated this conversation and that we have said 'Tell me — I want to hear what you want from us' makes the relationship between us much easier right from the start. It helps us to show the woman that we are on her side.

There needs to be a place in the notes to write the woman's needs and wants for labour. In the future, the notes will be a dialogue between the woman and the providers of care, with half the notes written by the care providers and the other half by the woman — a sort of diary of her pregnancy, her hopes for her labour, her decisions about feeding the baby, her feelings about her labour, towards the baby about herself as a mother, her evaluation of the service we are providing and her suggestions for future improvements. Until that day comes, however, here on the next page is an example of a card called a Programme for Pregnancy which is given to all women who go to one of the London teaching hospitals. On the other side of the card (not shown) are a list of recommended books, a space for 'Requests for My Birth Plan' and a list of what to bring in to hospital when the woman arrives in labour.

Finally the woman is asked.

Is there anything else you would like me to write down about you? If you think of anything else that you want to add during the next few months, tell us and we'll add it.

IS THIS THE BEST WAY TO GO ABOUT PREGNANCY?

So far I have discussed how a midwife can increase a woman's self-confidence when the pregnant woman is going to come to a

ANTENATAL   CLINIC   VISITS

16 Weeks — At the Hospital.

This week the Nurse will test my urine

The Doctor or Midwife will measure my Blood Pressure

Check for swelling of fingers or ankles

Weigh me ☐

Examine my abdomen ☐

Questions I want to ask this week:-

20 Weeks — At your G.P.'s Surgery or at the Hospital with either a Doctor or Midwife.

Urine test ☐   Weight ☐   Blood Pressure ☐   Abdomen ☐
Swelling ☐

Can I feel the baby move yet?

Questions I want to ask this week:—

24 Weeks — At your G.P.'s Surgery or at the Hospital with either a Doctor or Midwife.

Urine test ☐   Weight ☐   Blood Pressure ☐   Abdomen ☐
Swelling ☐

Questions I want to ask this week:-

28 Weeks — At the Hospital. A long visit today.

Urine test ☐   Blood test for anaemia ☐

Discussion with the Midwife about feeding the baby and how to prepare my Breasts ☐

Discussion with the Midwife about Classes ☐

My first class starts on . . . .

The Midwife will give me a Certificate of Expected Confinement (MAT B1) and will explain how to apply for Maternity benefits.

Swelling ☐   Weight ☐   Blood Pressure ☐   Abdomen ☐
Questions:

30 Weeks — At your G.P.'s Surgery or at the Hospital with either a Doctor or Midwife.

Urine test ☐   Weight ☐   Blood Pressure ☐   Abdomen ☐
Swelling ☐
Questions:

32 Weeks — At the Hospital with either a Doctor or Midwife

Urine test ☐   Weight ☐   Blood Pressure ☐   Abdomen ☐
Swelling ☐
Questions: Discuss analgesia ☐

34 Weeks — With your G.P. or at the Hospital with either a Doctor or Midwife.

Urine test ☐   Weight ☐   Blood Pressure ☐   Abdomen ☐
Swelling ☐
Questions:

36 Weeks — At the Hospital with your Consultant Obstetrician.

Urine test ☐   Weight ☐   Blood Pressure ☐   Abdomen ☐
Swelling ☐
Blood Test for anaemia ☐
Questions:

37 Weeks — At Hospital with Midwife/Doctor.

Urine test ☐   Weight ☐   Blood Pressure ☐   Abdomen ☐
Swelling ☐
Discussion about labour ☐   Birth Plan completed ☐
Questions:

38 Weeks — At the Hospital with a Doctor.

Urine test ☐   Weight ☐   Blood Pressure ☐   Abdomen ☐
Swelling ☐
Questions:

39 Weeks — At Hospital with Doctor/Midwife

Urine test ☐   Weight ☐   Blood Pressure ☐   Abdomen ☐
Swelling ☐
Questions:

40 Weeks — At the Hospital with a Doctor.

Urine test ☐   Weight ☐   Blood Pressure ☐   Abdomen ☐
Swelling ☐
Questions:

41 Weeks — At the Hospital with a Doctor

Urine test ☐   Weight ☐   Blood Pressure ☐   Abdomen ☐
Swelling ☐
Questions:

hospital antenatal clinic. I have also illustrated a chart which details an expected 13 visits to an antenatal care provider by the pregnant woman. Are these visits helpful? Are they useful? If we expect the woman to be at the antenatal clinic for a minimum of 30 minutes and if we note that it probably takes her an hour each time she comes (taking into account her travelling time and her extra journeys or extra waiting to have an ultrasound scan), we are talking about hours and hours of women's time. For what? Does all this antenatal care really guarantee a healthy baby? Will any intra-uterine growth retardation be picked up? If it is, what can be done about it? Can you help me to have a normal-sized baby if you detect that the baby inside me is too small? What about high blood pressure? Is the measurement taken in the clinic accurate after I have waited for an hour or more?

If I were spending this amount of time at a language class or car maintenance class, I should expect to have learnt a new language or at least some new skills after expending that amount of time. Do the women we see benefit from their antenatal visits?

The Black Report showed us that despite the increase in hospital care of pregnant women and the high level of medical and midwifery input in the antenatal period, the neonatal mortality rates of babies born to women in social class 5 are twice those in social class 1. We have known for a long time that the people who do not take up the antenatal services we offer are from the poorer socioeconomic groups. So is the hospital antenatal clinic catering for a group which does not need its services anyway?

Midwives involved with antenatal care would benefit from reading the work of Marion Hall, who in 'Effectiveness and Satisfaction in Antenatal Care', a paper given with Pang K. Chng, says: 'We call into question the efficacy and cost-effectiveness of routine antenatal care.' This paper and her papers in *The Lancet* and *British Medical Journal* in 1980 show that intra-uterine growth retardation is overdiagnosed. For every seven women who were told they had it, with all the attendant anxiety the diagnosis brings, only two actually delivered a growth-retarded baby. Furthermore, less than half of the women who actually delivered small-for-dates babies were diagnosed prior to their labour.

Raised blood pressure was also overdiagnosed. With this

diagnosis came the risks of increased induction and admission to hospital and an increase in the anxiety of the woman. For every seven women diagnosed as having high blood pressure in the antenatal clinic, only three actually had a real raised blood pressure.

The Royal College of Obstetricians and Gynaecologists have also been influenced by Marion Hall's work, and in its publication, 'Report of a Working Party on Antenatal and Intrapartum Care', suggests the following regime for pregnant women:

		Seen by
At 12 weeks	The pregnant woman is booked for care and confinement and determination of gestation.	*Obstetrician*
At 16–18 weeks	For alphafetoprotein screening and other blood tests.	GP or Midwife
At 22 weeks	For baseline weight for IUGR prediction.	GP or Midwife
At 26 weeks	Primigravidae only.	GP or Midwife
At 30 weeks	For selection for IUGR and pregnancy-induced hypertension screening.	Obstetrician
At 34 weeks	Primigravidae only.	GP or Midwife
At 36 weeks	For detection of malpresentation and PIH screening.	GP or Midwife
At 38 weeks	Primigravidae only.	GP or Midwife
At 40 weeks	For assessment of delivery.	Obstetrician

So having cut down the visits to the hospital as much as possible and having tried to make at least the first visit a more positive experience for the pregnant woman, I still ask should she be at the hospital at all? Many women will want to be there. But what about the woman who wants to have her baby at home? Should she be there? Why is she there?

Often the woman goes to the hospital because, when she went to see her GP and said that she would like to have her baby at home, she was told that the GP did not do home deliveries, or that they are not done nowadays, or that he would not let his wife have one. In the gentle vulnerable frame of mind most pregnant women are in, she allowed herself to be booked in at the hospital. But if this woman wants to have her baby at home, it is her choice. Furthermore, it is a perfectly responsible choice if she falls into the category of low risk — which 85% of women do. Evidence is increasing that having a baby at home may be safer for the low risk woman than having the baby in hospital.

In the *British Medical Journal* of 22 September 1984, Rona Campbell and colleagues examine the 8856 births which took place in the home in 1979. They come to the conclusion that the perinatal mortality among births booked to occur at home is low, especially for parous women. The perinatal mortality rate was 4·1/1000 for babies of women booked to give birth at home. Campbell admits that in this survey they do not know what happened to the roughly 10% of women who were booked to give birth at home but who were transferred to hospital in labour. However, she suggests that even including these transfers, the perinatal mortality rate for women booked for home delivery would probably only have been about 8/1000 compared to the national figure in 1979 of 14·6/1000.

In the *Journal of the Royal College of General Practitioners* of August 1984, S. M. I. Damstra-Wijmenga compares what happened to 1692 mothers who gave birth in Groningen (Holland) in 1981. He examines the 88% of low-risk women who could choose whether to have their babies at home or in hospital and compares what happened to those who decided to give birth at home to those who decided to give birth in hospital. Of the women who decided to give birth at home, two out of three primiparae and six out of seven multiparae actually gave birth at home. Damstra-Wijmenga shows that the women who booked for home delivery developed significantly fewer complications during pregnancy, labour and the puerperium than the women who chose hospital. Furthermore, the morbidity among their babies was lower than that of the babies of the women who opted for hospital. He surmises that in a hospital or maternity clinic the very surroundings and equipment may give rise to iatrogenic complications.

In the *British Journal of Obstetrics and Gynaecology* of February 1983, Michael Klein comes to a similar conclusion. He compares two groups of women. In one group the women were booked for a shared care system with the consultant obstetric unit. In the other they were booked for a general practitioner unit and received a significant amount of their care in labour while they were at home. Klein finds a disproportionate number of complications occurring in the women delivered in the consultant obstetric unit. He suggests that this might be due to the inappropriateness of using skills that should be saved for high-risk mothers on low-risk mothers.

Marjorie Tew has for years analysed published statistics and, in her paper in *The Place of Birth*, she again shows that the home is a safe option for low-risk women and that, in fact, hospital delivery may increase the risk to women who have no need of highly specialised services.

Having discovered that a woman wants to have her baby at home, what is the sensitive and caring midwife to do? With whom should she stand? Should she tell the woman that she would never let her daughter/sister/self have a home delivery or should she be 'with woman' as her name implies?

In areas where the community midwifery service is strong, midwives keep the telephone number of the community midwifery nursing officer at hand so that they can ring her and book the woman in for a visit by the community midwives prior to a booking for a home birth. In some areas where the service is not strong, the midwives keep a list of GPs who will book the woman for a home birth. Other midwives, whose service is in an even sadder state, keep the telephone number of their local NCT or birth centre group. They can refer the woman to them so that the group can support her through her negotiations for getting a home birth. And finally, some midwives keep handy the telephone number of a woman they know who had a baby at home. They ring her to ask her to help the woman to achieve a birth at home and to put the woman in touch with whatever networks there are among women to try to organise home births. In these cases, the supportive women are really taking over the role of the supportive midwife because a supportive midwife is not available.

Some areas have a general practitioner unit where mothers can give birth in a more relaxed setting than the normal busy obstetric unit. If there is one in your area, the woman you are booking may not know this. She may also not know that it is her choice whether she has shared care with her GP or not (as long as the GP can offer it).

Domino (domiciliary in and out) deliveries are frequently talked about as the ideal for the low risk woman but they have never really taken off, and the number done annually is at a very generous estimate not more than 3·5% of all births. In theory a domino delivery works as follows. The woman books with her local community midwife, who sees her (usually at the GP's clinic) throughout her pregnancy. When the woman goes into labour, she rings her midwife who comes to her home and supervises the beginning of the labour in the home. They then move to the hospital for the actual delivery. After the birth, if all is well, the woman rests in hospital for 6–24 hours and is then transferred back home to the care of her midwife again.

It sounds lovely for both mother and midwife, and it has been hailed as the 'safe' alternative to home deliveries by those who are afraid of home deliveries. Indeed it can be a lovely way to have a baby, but the many disadvantages of the scheme should be acknowledged. Many units are no longer 'allowing' a community midwife to stay on call for women whom she has come to know during pregnancy. The labouring women have to have the midwife who is actually on call. Whether any authority can actually change so drastically the working practice of a professional person to the detriment of the client and of the giver of care has not yet been challenged, and this very punitive regime *should* be challenged because it is not in the interest of either the patient or the midwife. Ultimately it means that the woman who has come to know her own midwife may end up being delivered by a total stranger.

Some midwives find it very frustrating to move a woman when she is getting into her labour, going inside herself, dilating beautifully, when it would be better for her to be left where she is, and when it is quite obvious to the midwife that the delivery will progress normally because of the feelings the midwife has about this labour.

Often problems crop up with the transfer of the woman home, especially if the health district decides that women having domino deliveries must go home by ambulance. This often means waiting hours for the ambulance to transfer the woman, which is very inconvenient for both mother and midwife. Many authorities, in these days of cuts, are encouraging women to go home in the family car. This is better in terms of convenience, provided, of course, that the family has a car.

I have painted a rather unsatisfactory picture of domino deliveries, so I want to add that when they work well, they can be very satisfying for both mother and midwife. There is continuity of care, combined with the relaxed atmosphere of home at the beginning of labour which the little group often seems able to take with them into the hospital labour ward, and then back home again soon afterwards.

The choices that a woman makes about her maternity care can have a huge influence on the outcome of her labour. When encouraging women to make out a birth plan, the work of Myra Snell is very useful.

The woman can be encouraged to consider how she feels about:

Who is coming with her when she has the baby. This can include the husband, partner, mother, mother-in-law, girl friend, daughter, son, her father or a priest.

How many people she wants with her.

What she wants in the way of light snacks during labour. It is probably better for her to bring these with her.

What she wants to wear during labour. What a woman has to wear during labour can have a very positive effect on the whole progress of her labour. When she wears her own clothes, she looks and feels like herself. I am sure this helps us to treat her in a more sensitive way. Often the clothes a woman brings into wear during labour allow her to be more mobile. If the hospital gown is one which opens down the back and half the ties are missing from it, ever time she tries to crawl her bottom will be exposed to the world. This is intimidating and embarrassing. I usually suggest that women bring with them an old nightdress or one of their husband's old T shirts or shirts, or even a maternity dress that they are fed up with wearing and do not mind getting a bit messed up during delivery. It does not matter what the garment is as long as it is clean.

Whether she would like to bring some of her own pillows in with her. When a woman brings in her own pillows in her own pillow cases, they make the beds in the delivery room and in the postnatal ward look more like her own bed. They also smell like her own pillows, and they are usually softer and more cosy than the plastic-covered pillows met in hospital.

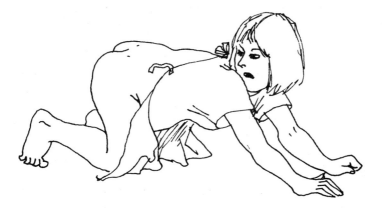

What entertainments she would like for labour. These can include a portable radio, cassette player, playing cards, scrabble, chess. All these will help to pass the time. Labour is nearly always longer than anyone ever anticipates.

Whether she would like to be ambulant during labour. When women are given the option of being on a bed for labour and delivery, many will choose to be on a bed. An equally large number, however, will want to try being ambulant for at least some if not all of their labour.

Whether she has any strong feelings about using a bedpan. Some women really cannot bear the thought of using a bedpan. There is usually nothing to stop them using the lavatory throughout their labour. They need, however, to have the implications of analgesia explained to them if they express horror at the thought of using a bedpan.

What she feels about the different analgesics available. The woman needs to know the pros and cons of each of the analgesics we offer. Please look at Table 1.

The Birth Plan can also consider how the woman feels about:

How the baby is delivered. Does she want the baby put straight on her abdomen? Or would she prefer it to be cleaned up first? What about the cord? Does she have any strong feelings about that?

Episiotomy — what are her feelings? Some women will say quite categorically that they would rather tear than have an

Table 1 Pros and cons of the analgesics used in labour

Pros	Cons
Pethidine	
● Good analgesia	● Women say they feel drunk.
● Seems to have a softening effect on cervix and to increase dilatation.	● Women say that it does not help much with relief of pain.
● Can give a woman a short 'time out' and a refreshing sleep.	● Women say that they feel in a drugged sea of pain.
● Some women like it very much.	
Pethidine plus phenergan/sparine	
● Seems to make the effect of pethidine greater.	● Women feel more drugged.
	● Amnesic effect — women forget their labours.
Epidurals	
● Woman is alert and bright.	● They do not always work.
● Very good analgesia.	● Greater risk of instrumental delivery.
● Good at lowering blood pressure.	● Loss of mobility.
● Good for instrumental delivery.	● ?increased pain of stitches afterwards.
	● If the epidural does not work, the woman is in a worse state than if she had not had one. Emotionally she has prepared herself for no pain and has 'softened up'. The pain appears worse than before.
Entonox	
● Self-administered.	● Smells unpleasant.
● Fairly good pain relief.	● Some women find it ineffective.
● Oxygenates the baby.	● Not very strong analgesia.
● No restriction on mobility as far as pipe will stretch. The woman can be standing up.	
● Quickly exhaled.	

episiotomy. Others will prefer not to have one but will leave it up to the midwife. I met one woman who positively wanted an episiotomy because she believed that it would be better for her pelvic floor muscles.

Syntometrine — does she have any strong feelings about its use?
Many women now are hoping to deliver without the use of syntometrine. They believe (quite rightly) that if it is used the third stage has to become a rushed procedure which then spoils the atmosphere of a beautiful calm delivery. Furthermore, they

are not prepared to put up with the extra nausea, afterpains and headaches that syntometrine can cause.

After delivery what does she want to happen? The woman can talk this through. She may be hoping for a quiet time with her baby and with her companions. She may want her other children to be brought to meet the baby immediately, or her parents or parents-in-law to come. She may be longing for a cup of tea and some toast or a cup of coffee and a Mars bar or champagne. She may welcome being blanket-bathed. She may prefer to get up to the bathtub. She may want to leave being washed until she has had a snooze. It is difficult to decide in advance but it opens the mind to possibilities, and if the woman has been encouraged to voice her likes and dislikes to us, it will make it easier for her to tell us during and after labour what she would prefer.

It is such a special day — more important than her wedding or her 21st birthday or any other important time in her life. We can make it shine out as a time of celebration — after all it is somebody's birthday!

Other midwives will think of other questions for the woman's birth plan. Myra Snell suggests that at the end you ask the women:

Will you take guidance from the midwife if at any time she is worried about the health and safety of your baby?

Helping a woman to be confident in herself involves listening to what a woman says, and to this end we have discussed helping her to think through many possibilities. The growth of her confidence, however, is also very affected by our words. For instance, when a woman comes to her very first antenatal appointment, she often has not yet 'told the world' about her pregnancy. She is waiting for our confirmation of the pregnancy. She needs to hear — 'Yes, you are pregnant. You are just the right size. Your blood pressure is excellent, and you are eating the right foods (after a discussion on diet).' At further visits she needs to hear us say something positive about the pregnancy *every time she comes.*

When we are working in a department day after day, we lose touch with the fact that this is a real occasion for the women who come, that when they get home their mother will ring up and say 'Well, what did they say to you at the clinic?', that in the evening her partner will be given a blow-by-blow account of the visit and that the following day at work all her colleagues will ask. She needs to be able to tell them that all is well. She will only be able to do that, however, if you have said something like:

- You are the right size.
- Your blood pressure is excellent.
- You are looking wonderful.
- Everything is going well.
- You've done so well to cut down to two a day. Congratulations.
- The baby feels just the right size.
- No you're not enormous. You're just the right size.
- No you're not too small. The baby feels just right.
- Carry on doing what you are doing. You've obviously got it right.
- The baby is a good size — just right for your pelvis.
- The baby is little and neat — just right for you.
- You are doing very well.

Never does one say 'The baby is enormous'. This is terrifying even to a large woman. Nor should one say 'I can't find the head', or 'It's got a big head'. Remember that the words you say to the woman today in an antenatal clinic will be quoted to her friends in ten, fifteen years time. Be careful with words. They are a very strong influence, both positive and negative.

CONDITIONS THAT CROP UP ANTENATALLY

Tiredness

The extreme exhaustion of the early days of pregnancy are almost crippling. Women can fall asleep over their desks. They often drag themselves home in the evening and have to go to bed immediately because they feel so utterly drained and exhausted. Their life takes on a work/sleep routine in which nothing else can be contemplated. Sometimes women feel so awful that they think they have some terrible wasting disease.

The exhaustion will pass away but it needs to be recognised as utterly draining for the first few months.

Headache

Many women experience blinding headaches at the beginning of pregnancy and may well need to have their eyes tested and to wear glasses during the pregnancy. It may be a type of migraine which can be exacerbated by pregnancy or it may be a result of the change in size of the eye from front to back which happens in pregnancy.

Spitting

Many women over-salivate at the beginning of pregnancy, and some find it exceedingly distressing. If you can find another woman with the same problem, they will gain enormous reassurance from each other.

Ligament pain

Many women feel a dull aching under their 'bump'. It is more common on the left side, but it can be on either side or both. It can be a sharp dragging pain, and it makes the woman feel

that she wants to support her abdomen as she walks along. It is thought to be due to the stretching of the round ligament as the uterus enlarges. It is more common in multigravid women than in primigravidae, but it can occur in both. The only advice that we can give is to suggest that the woman avoid pulling on these ligaments by keeping intra-abdominal pressure to a minimum. When she coughs or laughs, the woman should be encouraged to bend her knees, and when she gets up from a lying position, she should be encouraged to roll over onto her side and get up on her hands and knees. She might also find a maternity belt helpful.

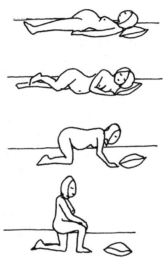

Varicosities

Varicose veins in pregnant women's legs are well documented. They should be treated with support stockings or tights and the woman advised to keep walking and to try to have her legs supported when she sits down. She should try not to sit with her legs hanging down and she should avoid standing for long periods.

The varicosities which worry women a great deal are the vulval varicosities — they feel so extraordinary, like a bunch of grapes underneath you. These varicosities ache and throb constantly. The woman is not comfortable standing or sitting. Lying down is the only time she gets any relief. Women who have this problem are usually multigravidae, but primigravid women are also often very conscious of the swelling of their vulva when the baby's head engages and both blood and lymphatic circulation from the vulva is hindered.

The woman with vulval varicosities needs to be reassured that during delivery the perineum is so stretched and thinned that the varicosities disappear — never to return again or, at least, not until the next pregnancy. They do not in anyway hamper delivery of the baby and they do not cause any problems at delivery.

Haemorrhoids

The woman may be aware of haemorrhoids every time she sits down. She can be shown how to push the haemorrhoid gently back inside her anus every time she has a bath. Treatment during pregnancy, however, is really only palliative because the haemorrhoids will remain until the birth of the baby. She can be shown the positive (!) side of haemorrhoids in that haemorrhoids indicate that she is producing plenty of progesterones which is the hormone that softens and relaxes tissues. This should mean that the birth of her baby should be that much easier and smoother.

The action of progesterone has other effects on the pregnant woman. Her limbs seem less under control than usual. She will suddenly 'go over' on her ankle for no reason. She may find that she has more falls than she has experienced since she was a child. She may find that she drops things, especially food down her front, but also crockery and other objects.

Position of the baby

One of the disadvantages of our very static culture — sitting in front of the television, driving to the shops, going on the bus, not having a garden — appears to be an increase in babies who start off in labour in a posterior position (see Ina May Gaskin's figures in *Spiritual Midwifery*) especially among primigravid women. The midwifery team that I work with has taken to suggesting to women that they should crawl for about ten minutes a day from 36 weeks of pregnancy onwards. We think that gravity may rotate the baby into an anterior position.

Many of the women ignore our advice because crawling is very boring, but some comply. For some women in labour, crawling is actually a very comfortable position and it may help to rotate the baby into an anterior position. Hopefully this is something we shall evaluate after we have done our present research.

Nausea

'Morning sickness' can often be evening sickness or even all day sickness, and for some women it does not go away after three months but lasts the duration of pregnancy. An in depth discussion with the woman about what she is eating will often reveal that she is taking in just about enough to keep her nourished during her pregnancy. All in all, it is a very miserable situation. She needs support and encouragement and if possible someone else to talk to who has or had the same problem. Women often find for themselves something that helps, such as acid fruits like plums or dry biscuits or toast — but sometimes nothing helps.

BENEFITS OF ANTENATAL CARE

Antenatal care can bring many benefits. It has the potential to be the first real educational experience that a woman has. It can be an enormously pleasant social occasion. It can be a time when she makes long-lasting and important friendships.

We as midwives can help women to get to know each other. We can have coffee morning-type meetings during an antenatal clinic. We can introduce women who live near each other and try to facilitate easy relationships between them. We can introduce topics to be discussed. We can show films with discussion sessions afterwards. We can hold meetings in the clinic during the evenings on such topics as:

Pain Relief: A Talk by an Anaesthetist
Also present will be four mothers who have recently had babies and have used each different type of analgesic. For the last hour of the session you will be able to discuss their experiences with them.

Different Ways of Giving Birth: Discussion with a Midwife
How do you want it to be?

Life after Birth: What is it Like?
Small discussion groups with new parents.

Feeding your Baby: Breast or Bottle?
An opportunity to meet mothers who have done both and to set up a contact with a breastfeeding counsellor.

All the suggestions I am making are within the province of a midwife who looks upon herself almost as a 'social secretary' for the women she is caring for. At the moment we can show precious little to be gained from the antenatal care we give, but if we can help a woman to find a friend and companion who lives near her and if we have helped her to set up her own support group among women going through the same experience, we have indeed given her something of very real value which will help and support her for years to come.

Having explored whether the most useful part a midwife can play antenatally may be a social role, it still behoves us to do a physical check on the woman — to take her blood pressure, test her urine, weigh her, check her for oedema, palpate her abdomen, enquire about fetal movements, diet, sleep, rest, thoughts, worries and so on, and to enable her to get to know us, her friend on the inside.

If midwives are to improve the experience of women at an antenatal clinic, it is important that they 'take on' some of the women coming to their clinic, that they take responsibility for a known group of women. If each midwife has an appointment diary, she can make realistic appointments for the women she is caring for. It makes great sense for more women to be seen by midwives, and I do not only mean the eight or so seen in the midwives clinic. They have an inordinate amount of time spent on them because there are so few women attending.

Let us imagine a hospital where there are 3500 deliveries a year. We will say that two-thirds of the women will be having shared care with their GP and community midwife, thus we are left with:

2333 who will only be coming about 3 times = 6999 visits

1167 who will be coming about 14 times = 16 338 visits

Total number of anticipated antenatal visits = 23 337 a year

Number per week = 449

If this number of women is divided up sensibly, we are only seeing 90 women a day. One doctor and four midwives could give each woman a 20-minute appointment and still each have two hours left at the end of an eight-hour day.

Doctor Day: Midwife Bay: Midwife Gay: Midwife Fay: Midwife Ray each have an appointment arranged for:

9.00
9.20
9.40
10.00
10.20
10.40 Break
11.00
11.20
11.40
12.00
12.20
12.40
13.00 Break
13.40
14.00
14.20
14.40
15.00
15.20
15.40
16.00

With this system, 95 women are seen in an unhurried manner — pleasant for both mother and care giver.

If a midwife has her own appointment diary and sees a group of women through their pregnancy, she will gain in confidence because of the affection which will develop between her and the women and because of her growing realisation that these women are coming to see her and that they are flourishing under her supportive care. Many midwives need help to regain their confidence after years of having their skills underutilised. The easiest way to help a midwife's confidence to grow is for her to start at the beginning of a pregnancy and follow the woman all the way through. The woman trusts 'her' midwife, so she will be able to talk to the midwife much more easily and will tell her of any untoward happenings. Her care is much 'safer' than seeing different people each time, no matter how eminent those people are. What choices do women have? They have precious few if midwives do not point them out to them. What choices do midwives have? They will only discover their choices when they really get to know a small group of women and follow them through their pregnancy, labour and puerperium. They will also discover their worth as midwives, how women need them and care about them, and the midwife's unique position and role in society. Looking after a friend throughout this huge experience is mind blowing. We do not usually have many friends who are having babies so it is imperative that we make friends with the women we are providing care for. From them we shall learn so much and from their love and affection we shall become stronger. Mothers need midwives, but midwives need mothers even more. We are both on the same side. We are both going through the same struggles and the same experience.

References and Further Reading

Campbell, R., MacDonald Davies, I., MacFarlane, A., Beral, V. (1984). Home Births in England and Wales, 1979: Perinatal mortality according to intended place of delivery. *British Medical Journal*; 289: 721–4 (September).

Central Midwives Board, Central Midwives Board for Scotland, Northern Ireland Council for Nurses & Midwives, and An Bord Altranais. (1983). *The Role of the Midwife*.

Damstra-Wijmenga, S. M. I. (1984). Home confinement: the positive results in Holland. *Journal of the Royal College of General Practitioners*; 34(265): 425–31 (August).

Gaskin, I. M. (1978). *Spiritual Midwifery*. Summertown: The Book Publishing Company. Available from The Book Publishing Company, The Farm, 156 Drakes Lane, Summertown, TN 38483 USA).

Hall, M., Chng, P. K. (1982). Antenatal care in practice. In *Effectiveness and Satisfaction in Antenatal Care*. Edited by Murray Enkin & Iain Chalmers. Published by Spastics International Medical Publications 1982.

Klein, M., Lloyd, I., Redman, C., Bull, M., Turnbull, A. C. (1983). A comparison of low-risk women booked for delivery in two systems of care: shared-care (consultant) and integrated general practice unit. I. Obstetrical procedures and neonatal outcome. II. Labour and delivery management and neonatal outcome. *British Journal of Obstetrics and Gynaecology*; 90: 118–22 and 123–8 (February).

Royal College of Obstetricians and Gynaecologists (1982). *Report of the RCOG Working Party on Antenatal and Intrapartum Care.* London: RCOG.

Snell, M. (1983). A Plan for Birth. *Nursing Times*; 79(7): 62–3 (February 16).

Tew, M. (1985). Place of birth and perinatal mortality. *Journal of the Royal College of General Practitioners*; 35(277): 390–4.

Townsend, P., Davidson, N. (1982). *Inequalities in Health. The Black Report.* Published by Penguin 1982.

Chapter Three

Pre-labour

The most common phenomenon to characterise labour is that the labour is not established labour. It is extremely common for women to have strong, painful, regular contractions during the last four weeks of pregnancy and for them to think, quite reasonably, that they are in labour. These contractions may last for a few hours, all night, two days or some part of most days, but they do not achieve any cervical dilatation. They appear to be some sort of 'limbering up' in a uterus which is 'irritable'. They come regularly, they are painful, they stop women from sleeping, and they are a nuisance because, having thought that she was in labour for about 12–24 hours, a woman is devasted to discover that she is not in established labour at all — that she is still at square one, tired, dejected and fed-up.

I shall never forget a woman who was expecting her second baby and whom I looked after when I was a district midwife. She rang me almost every day for the fortnight preceding the birth. Every morning at about 6 a.m. the telephone would ring and a very 'in labour' voice would say, 'Hello, Caroline. It's Marjorie here. I've been having contractions every ten minutes since 3 a.m. and I think *this is it*'.

I would then pull my clothes on and leap into the car and make my way to her house, I would be greeted by her looking very sheepish on the doorstep and saying 'I'm terribly sorry. They stopped the minute I put the telephone down'. Marjorie had contractions really strongly and regularly for long periods for a fortnight before her labour proper began. When she finally went into labour, her cervix was 4 cm dilated, she took another six hours to reach full dilation, and her beautiful second son was born 15 minutes later. Since Marjorie, I have met a huge number of women who have painful, regular Braxton Hicks contractions before labour starts, often from four weeks before the birth. It is more common, I think, in multiparous women but primigravid women also experience it.

In his book *Active Management of Labour*, Kieran O'Driscoll says: 'The most important single item in the management of labour is diagnosis. When the initial diagnosis is wrong, all subsequent management is likely to be wrong also, with unfortunate consequences which are seen almost daily in our delivery units, although seldom recognized for what they are. In medical circles, there is an almost universal failure to appreciate that the diagnosis of labour presents a genuine problem in everyday practice.'

This chapter is dedicated to every midwife who has spent the whole night with someone who is having strong regular contractions and, in the cold light of dawn, has realised that the 3 cm dilation of the cervix of 11 p.m. the evening before has not progressed at all and that they all need to go home and get some sleep in case the same happens again that evening. The only problem for the midwife is that she usually has to go to work, and so if the same does happen that evening she may well feel like a drained rag.

But take heart. In the same way that the woman in labour is never sent more than she can bear, nor is the midwife. She may be stretched to the limits of her endurance but she will always be able to dip into the deep well of her resources which are constantly replenished by good deliveries and love from her friends and patients.

The woman having regular and strong Braxton Hicks contractions is not the only problem midwives are confronted with when they are diagnosing labour. There is also the problem of ruptured membranes. If there has been a gush of amniotic fluid, there is no doubt as to whether the membranes have ruptured or not. Much more frequent, however, are the slight 'leaking', which indicates a hind water rupture which usually repairs itself if left alone, and the increase in vaginal discharge which precedes the onset of labour. A woman giving a history of a definite 'pop' inside her has usually ruptured her membranes. If she has no contractions, she is still not in labour, and the health of her baby is only put in jeopardy by a vaginal examination (whether by a gloved hand or by a speculum). This woman should not be in a labour ward. The most sensible place for her is resting and eating nourishing food either in her own home, where the risk of infection is minimal, or in an antenatal ward if the possibility of rest at home is unlikely.

Hind water rupture — when the bag of membranes ruptures somewhere behind the baby's head and amniotic fluid trickles out when the woman moves, when she goes upstairs or when she coughs — is a precursor to labour but is insignificant on its own. Usually the hindwater rupture heals itself in a day or two and no more amniotic fluid leaks out. Labour starts spontaneously a few days or weeks later and during the course of the labour the membranes rupture spontaneously. I have met many doctors who do not 'believe in' hind water rupture, but I feel that this is like saying that you do not 'believe in' the Forth Bridge or Westminster Abbey. Rupture of membranes is probably best left alone to await events.

Having dealt with the woman who has ruptured membranes, who will either eventually go into spontaneous labour or will be induced with syntocinon, we still need to look at the woman who is having strong contractions which are not producing any cervical dilatation. First and perhaps most important, she should *not* be on a labour ward. Labour wards are for women who are in established labour. Nothing is more demoralising than being on a labour ward — hearing women in the extremes of labour, hearing the crying of new-born babies, and being aware of the passing of day and night and of how everyone else but you has had their baby despite your wishing and longing for labour to get going. Even the kind enquiry 'Still here Mrs Jones?' is enough to fill the woman with despair. The woman having painful Braxton Hicks contractions is best off at home under the watchful surveillance of her local midwife. Failing that she can be on the antenatal ward, but the antenatal ward is very much second best — full of other people, with an atmosphere of hospitals, sickness and women having problems with their pregnancies. In such a pathological atmosphere, it is hard for a woman to remember and keep in touch with the normality of what she is experiencing. It is also hard for the midwives and doctors caring for her to remember this too.

A woman who presents with painful contractions is only in established labour if she has cervical dilatation of or exceeding 3 cm. If after four hours there is no progression from 3 cm, then it is unlikely that she is in established labour. The best place to be treating painful Braxton Hicks contractions is in the woman's home. One suggestion might be for her to go for a brisk walk which will either help to distract her from the contractions or bring them on much more strongly and efficiently.

Another way of relieving the very real pain of these contractions is for the woman to take two paracetamol tablets with a hot milky drink followed by a warm or hot bath. A stiff alcoholic drink of brandy, whisky or sherry can be a great help. Cider, wine or beer are also good.

Often the best way to deal with this 'false labour' is to try and encourage it to 'go away'. There is no use encouraging labour if it has not really started — labour never came with wishing. So one very good way for a woman to cope with these irritating and painful contractions is simply to sleep, if she can manage to do so.

On the other hand, if labour has started but has slowed down enormously and the woman is reluctant to have a syntocinon drip, there are several options to help to release natural oxytocin and get the labour going again. These are nipple stimulation, masturbation and sexual intercourse.

Nipple stimulation can be done either by hand or mouth, and probably the best person to do it is the woman's partner. If the relationship between the midwife and the couple is such that she can suggest this, she needs to be able to ensure privacy which can be a problem in a modern labour ward. It may be necessary for her to sit outside the room 'on guard' so that nobody bursts in. It would be much simpler if there were locks on the insides of labour ward doors, but this will not happen until the labouring couple are seen as individuals deserving privacy and respect rather than as 'patients to be treated'. In many labour wards the only place a couple can be ensured some privacy is in the lavatory or, more usefully, in the bathroom. There the woman can lie in the bath and have her nipples carressed by her partner. The effects of this will be more dynamic if they are in the dark.If this is not possible, the woman can have a dark flannel over her eyes.

Sexual intercourse is also difficult to arrange in a modern labour ward. Sheila Kitzinger has always said, 'The room where the baby is born should be the room in which it was or could have been conceived'. She means that the conditions which are conducive to making love are the same conditions which a woman needs to give birth in — privacy, warmth, quietness, comfort and being with a loved partner. There is a good quantity of prostaglandin in semen. Also the thrusting of the penis against the cervix helps the woman to release prostaglandin, and this can be a much more pleasant way to stimulate labour, much cheaper and less sore than prostaglandin pessaries or syntocinon.

Masturbation during labour can help to get a slow labour going, and it seems also to be a very good form of pain relief. It can also be done easily in a modern labour ward by the woman herself under a sheet so that a person coming into the room unexpectedly (the bugbear of the modern labour ward) need not know what is going on. It needs to be looked at as a benefit during labour but I cannot see any reasonable research getting underway until there is some privacy in the labour ward.

Kissing is also very useful in loosening the woman up and helping labour along, especially when it is on the lips by her partner. But it also helps her to be kissed on her arm or cheek by her midwife. Many midwives will have been surprised to find themselves giving hugs and kisses quite automatically to the woman they are with. The release of loving and caring feelings cannot help but smooth the path of labour, as labour is so susceptible to atmosphere.

Michael Klein *et al.* in the *British Journal of Obstetrics and Gynaecology* of February 1983 look at a system in which women who are booked for the general practitioner delivery unit are kept at home while in early labour for longer than women who are having shared care with their GP. The women who are kept at home for longer are those for whom the community midwife supervises the early stages of labour in their home or who go to their doctor's surgery and are advised from there.

The results of this research were that the women having shared care with their GP but delivering in the consultant unit were in hospital for longer — eleven hours compared with eight hours for primiparae, and six hours compared with four hours for multiparae. The implications of the longer period in hospital for this low risk group of women were that they had:

- More pethidine.
- More epidurals.
- More fetal monitoring.
- More augmentation with syntocinon.
- More forceps deliveries.

The implications for their babies were that:

- They more often had an Apgar score of less than 6.
- They were more likely to be intubated.

There were significant benefits for the women booked for care in the general practitioner unit, of whom 61·9% of primiparae and 33·3% of multiparae had a home visit from a midwife, despite the fact that they actually laboured for longer than their sisters in the shared care system.

- They spent less time in the labour ward.
- They had less pethidine.
- They had fewer epidurals.
- They received less electronic fetal monitoring.
- They received less augmentation with syntocinon.
- They had more normal deliveries and fewer forceps deliveries.
- Their babies had higher Apgar scores.
- None of their babies needed intubating.

Damastra-Wijmenga's work, which I have already referred to in Chapter 1, is very relevant here and is worth looking at again and in more detail. Damstra-Wijmenga describes what happened to 1692 women in Groningen in Holland when they gave birth in 1981. The women were divided into four categories:

a)   Mothers who had opted for home confinement.
b)   Mothers who had opted for hospital confinement followed by a 24 hour stay.
c)   Mothers who had opted for hospital confinement followed by a stay of seven days.
d)   Mothers who had to be closely supervised by an obstetrician from the start of pregnancy and had to deliver in hospital due to an increased risk (primary medical indication).

The mothers in groups a, b and c were considered to be 'low risk' pregnant women.

The women in group d had no choice as to where they could have their babies — they were deemed to be 'high risk' and they delivered in hospital. This group was not studied. The women in the other three groups were given the choice of delivering either in hospital or at home. If they chose hospital, they could further choose to stay for either 24 hours or seven days.

Damstra-Wijmenga says that of the women choosing to have their babies at home, 77% actually delivered there. These women developed fewer complications during pregnancy, labour and the puerperium and their babies had lower morbidity than the women in groups b and c. He surmises that 'The increasing medicalization of obstetrics has given rise to the notion that it would be "safer" to deliver in hospital. The safety aspect is emphasised in many publications, both in the professional literature and the lay press. The fact that in a hospital or maternity clinic the very surroundings and equipment may give rise to iatrogenic complications is apparently overlooked.'

I suggest that everyone with experience of looking after pregnant women would agree that women who are not in established labour should be at home and not in a labour ward or even in the pathological atmosphere of an antenatal ward. How much more humane it is when women who are in false or early labour can be at home with the reassurance of friendly and knowledgeable visits from the community midwife. How much more cost effective and safe it is to have women who are not in labour kept away from the labour ward and not subjected to stimulation of the uterus with its accompanying dangers of increased pain, prolonged labour, greater use of analgesia and greater need for instrumental delivery. I remember the sensitive words of Desmond Barden, speaking at the twenty-fifth conference of the Association for Improvements in the Maternity Service. He described the genetically-transmitted knowledge that women have about giving birth. He contrasted this with the meeting of 'two near paralytic drunks' which is how he described the first meeting of the over-sedated mother and her equally over-sedated baby.

Labour is very painful when it happens at home, in familiar surroundings, with the woman feeling secure, with people around her who love her and who she also loves and trusts, with furniture against which is easy for her to be mobile and flexible. The pain is enormously increased by the fear induced by uncomfortable 'delivery beds', total strangers, strange manipulations of her body, and lack of privacy. We have much to be responsible for when we allow women to labour in such antipathetic surroundings.

It is only midwives, aware of what is hapening, who can fashion labour wards which are sensitive to the needs of women, which are safe and secure, which are places of love and respect for women, where women can labour in dignity, safety, privacy and comfort. The labour ward needs to be perceived as the woman's room — where no one would dream of entering without being invited, where the woman can roam about using different pieces of furniture or soft mats to gain the most comfort while she is in labour, where the baby can be monitored with a Pinard's stethoscope, a sonicaid or telemetry if absolutely necessary, where the woman can spend hours in a large bath of water if she so desires, where she can have with her those people she loves, where light and sound can be excluded, where the midwife can sit comfortably throughout the labour without feeling impelled to 'do' something and simply aware of the value of her just 'being there', where the woman is the prime reason for everyone's existence, where she is the paramount, 'the queen' for that day.

It is up to midwives to bring about these changes — they require very little in the way of expensive equipment but a very great deal in terms of changes of emphasis and perception.

References and Further Reading

Bardon, D. (1985). Speaking at the 25th Birthday Conference of the Association for Improvements in the Maternity Services on November 29, 1985.

Damstra-Wijmenga, S. M. I. (1984). Home confinement: the positive results in Holland. *Journal of the Royal College of General Practitioners*; 34(265): 425–31 (August).

Klein, M., Lloyd, I., Redman, C., Bull, M., Turnbull, A. C. (1983). A comparison of low-risk women booked for delivery in two systems of care: shared-care (consultant) and integrated general practice unit. I. Obstetrical procedures and neonatal outcome. II. Labour and delivery management and neonatal outcome. *British Journal of Obstetrics and Gynaecology*; 118–22 and 123–8 (February).

O'Driscoll, K., Meagher D. (1980). *Active Management of Labour*. Philadelphia: W. B. Saunders Company Ltd.

Chapter Four

Labour

When does labour start? In Chapter 3 we looked at the woman who seems to be starting labour several times before labour really gets going. What about the majority of women? What is their experience?

During the run up to labour the body gives many signs of loosening up with the influence of progesterone. Many women feel loose and somehow 'disjointed'. The floor is so far away that they leave things they have dropped for their husband to pick up when he comes in. Their joints feel stiff and out of control when they get up in the morning, and often they feel very stiff when they begin to walk.

Many women experience difficulty in sleeping during the last few weeks of pregnancy. They are awakened frequently by the need to urinate. They awake sweating from vivid and horrible nightmares or disturbing daydreams. They frequently 'know' in their bones that it is going to happen next Saturday and, when it does not, they are depressed and irritable with everyone and everything around them.

In the later stages of pregnancy, women cannot concentrate. They cannot read a book. They find it difficult to focus on a serious television programme. The more intelligent woman can be quite despairing that her mind has gone for ever. She hates the fact that she runs upstairs to fetch something, but cannot remember what it was when she gets there.

Towards the end of pregnancy many women excrete large globs of jelly-like mucus from their vagina. They experience urinary frequency because of the pressure of the baby's head on their bladder. Their vulva swells to vast proportions. They get many twinges and contractions. Often they have a show, and usually they have diarrhoea for a couple of days prior to the onset of labour.

For many women the first contractions of labour bring a feeling of euphoria and excitement, mixed with nervousness about what is to come. Each contraction is timed both for length and for space between. The partner is alerted. The mother and mother-in-law are told. The whole family is on the alert.

I always try to cool the situation by pointing out that a first labour usually lasts at least 24 hours, that this could well be a false alarm, that the woman should ignore this part and get on with her ironing, watching the television, going for a walk, cooking the lunch, painting the nursery and so on. She should continue her normal life as much as possible, keeping herself well nourished with little snacks and having frequent naps so as not to get overtired. This is important because this part of labour, the pre-labour phase, can last for one or two days. On the other hand it can get going quite rapidly, but as long as she is bouncing around saying brightly and excitedly 'Oooo it does hurt, but I thought it would be worse than this, I wonder how much longer I've got. When do you think it will come? Have you packed your Mars bar?' and other such chat, nothing very dramatic is happening, and it is fine to be carrying on at home with everyday life as much as possible.

Throughout labour it is important for the woman to empty her bladder regularly. Her partner can be encouraged to take control of this and to remind her to urinate regularly every hour and a half. The skill of the midwife at this point is to be patient.

Her role is to sit quietly in a corner, perhaps knitting or reading, or perhaps just thinking about the woman and concentrating on her cervical dilatation, providing light snacks and sociably joining in.

The early 'chatty' part of labour is fun. It gives time for a midwife to build a relationship with the couple if she does not know them already, and it gives her a chance to prepare everything she is going to need for later. It is also her chance to create an atmosphere of peaceful confidence and for her to help the couple to make the labour room into their own place — their bedroom. For the more fortunate woman, this part of her labour will be spent at home with her local midwife keeping in touch, sometimes visiting, sometimes phoning up. (See the description of Klein's paper in Chapter 4.)

Women can be encouraged to make the room feel more like their own by keeping their own clothes on — a maternity dress that is easy to wash, one of their husband's shirts, a nightdress (as will be revealed later, it is more useful to have on ordinary clothes rather than nightclothes). Their own pillows and own pillowcases make the bed look and smell more like their own bed. Many women like to bring in a photo or two or a favourite picture to make the room more like home. A cassette player playing their favourite music can also help. Hearing a piece by Mozart always gives me a great rush of energy, but the same music does not appeal to everyone, and the midwife needs to be aware of what the music is doing to her too I find much Country and Western music and some of the more discordant recent music very sapping.

Another way of helping a woman to feel at home, and also an effective form of pain relief, is for the woman to lie in a warm bath for a good part of her labour. Many women find this immensely comforting and having a cup of tea or coffee in the bath can feel positively sybaritic.

In her preparation of the birth room, the midwife can also utilise whatever aids for comfort she has at her disposal in the labour ward. A soft 'physio' mat can be wonderful for the woman to crawl or lie on. Covered with a clean sheet, it is hygenic for delivery or vaginal examinations. The woman needs to be near the ground. She needs to be able to put her feet on the ground and get up and walk away. Even if she does not actually do this, it is important for her to feel that she can.

Research into the psychology of labour is in its infancy but I am sure that when we can really measure those things that cause real distress to women, we shall realise how cruel our present high beds have been for women. It is like putting her on a high shelf in view of everyone. She needs to be private, able to be active and restless, able to take up any position she feels comfortable in.

Bean bags are also wonderful because they adjust to her shape. She can drape herself, or lie back on them. In this position, she can see what is going on, it is easy to deliver her, and it is also easy for the midwife to perform a vaginal examination.

She can also lie forward on the bean bag with her abdomen supported. This helps to give the baby room to rotate if it is in a posterior position. It is marvellous if she has backache because her back is easily accessible for massaging. She can deliver easily and comfortably in this position. The midwife can also do vaginal examinations when the woman is in this position but

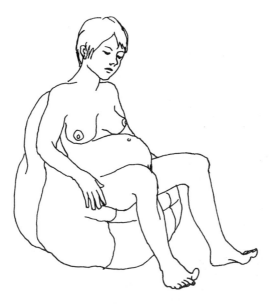

this can be more difficult and rather confusing as we are so used to doing them the other way up.

Some units have birthing beds which can adjust to different positions. Some of these beds are immensely useful and comfortable for the labouring woman but often they have been designed with the midwife rather than the woman in mind. Often they seem to be an attempt to give women more flexibility while still making sure they conform to our confinement of

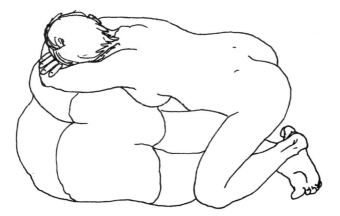

them. In many of these birthing beds a woman has no control over the angle at which she is sitting, and she has very restricted mobility — it is still *our* labour, we are still in control. Perhaps it is time we gave labour back to women.

The woman who has been chatting and excited up until now will gradually withdraw into herself. She will speak less and less. She will be concentrating on the sensations she is feeling inside herself.

Chat is now aggravating to her. If you are a stranger, she probably does not feel able to tell you to be quiet. It is up to the midwife to make sure that there is peace and quiet and that any student midwives or medical students are sitting quietly and comfortably. The more people in the room, the more difficult it is for the woman to concentrate on her labour and to surrender to it. One midwife and one student is really one too many but is something that the midwife and mother are usually prepared to accommodate in order for students to learn. Some students have so much empathy and so much instinctive feeling for the woman that they are a positive factor in a labour.

The woman goes inside herself. The contractions are stronger and longer and the space between them is getting shorter. The strength of the pain increases but the overwhelming sensation of labour is really that — an overwhelming *sensation*. The body is a huge throbbing entity entirely filled with sensation — feeling, being, hurting, hot, angry, loving — just pure feelings. This is why it is so uncomfortable for the woman to have these sensations disturbed. She needs to be able just to experience all of it in peace.

The hours tick by. Time goes by amazingly quickly during a labour — perhaps because of the feeling of timelessness. The woman is coping, but only just. The pain and the sensations are becoming overwhelming. She begins to moan — 'Caroline, I think I need an epidural. It's getting too much'. You know that she has always said that she does not want any analgesia if she can manage without. You know that this is important to her. This is the time to support her and give her some time out of this experience which is too much for her at this moment.

Now is the time for distraction. 'Jane, you haven't passed urine recently. Could you go and try and pass some, please? Keith, shall you go with her? I'll go and put the kettle on and we'll have some more tea.'

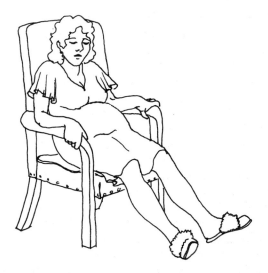

Jane staggers off to the lavatory, stopping to cope with each contraction as it comes. By the time she is back from urinating and is sitting in a chair (head above her uterus to increase her pain threshold), half an hour has gone by, the birth is half an hour nearer and probably the crisis is past. Jane is coping again. Perhaps now is the time for encouraging words

- That's right — you're doing it beautifully.
- You're wonderfully relaxed.
- Oh marvellous.
- Good, good, good.
- Oh you are so wonderful. That's right. Go with it.
- Surrender to it, surrender. Let it wash over you. Let it take you over.
- Keith, isn't she amazing? I've never seen anyone so relaxed.
- Doesn't she look beautiful — perfect relaxation.

A few kisses may help here too. We aim for an atmosphere of loving, caring and involved support.

The woman begins to go off into herself again. As she reaches another plane in her consciousness, it is thought that she releases endorphins — the naturally-occurring analgesic. She is helped to do this by darkness or very dimmed lights, lack of other stimuli, no noise, no strong smells, peacefulness.

She may moan or groan. This may upset you but it might be

just right for her and need no input from the midwife. Sometimes it may help to keep saying soothing words during a contraction so that she knows that you are still there and are with her in spirit. On the other hand, however, this may just be a comfort for you.

Another crisis may occur — another moment when an epidural/pethidine/a general anaesthetic/anything is requested in pitiful tones. You answer — 'Of course I'll go and get the anaesthetist, but first of all we must have your bladder empty, Jane, so could you go and do that, please? And then we shall need to change your clothes — out of your dress and into your delivery gown would be best.'

Contractions are coming thick and fast now. It takes Jane a long time to get to the lavatory as she leans against Keith for every contraction. In fact she may not feel that she can get there at all and she may need a bedpan. All this buys time. Often by this stage, if the fetal head is lower than the ischial spines, the woman will not be able to pass urine. Once that is over, it is time for her to get undressed and put on a delivery gown. This takes several more minutes as strong contractions are coming frequently. Then, obviously, before alerting the anaesthetist, it is important to perform a vaginal examination. Usually because of your delaying tactics, the most you are likely to feel will be a rim of cervix or at least 8 cm of cervical dilatation. Jane may be so bucked up by this news that she may feel that she will manage the short time left.

ANALGESIA

I am not a sadist. If a woman really needs some analgesia, there is a time and place for it. I remember vividly arguing with a new registrar last year. I was asking her to write up 150 mg of pethidine for a woman and she was refusing on the grounds that the accepted practice was to give only 100 mg. I finally managed to persuade her with the words, 'Look Doctor, in the past 12 months I have given pethidine on only two occasions. I don't overuse it, but in this case I know that this woman needs 150 mg rather than 100 mg'.

Often 50 mg of pethidine at the right moment can be a great help and relaxer, but it is a drug to be approached with great caution. Many women hate the effects of it. They say that it makes them feel drunk and out of control and that its pain-relieving qualities are very much overestimated. It can make the woman appear more comfortable and relaxed to onlookers but her memory can be of a drugged sea of pain if she has had too much. I would also very much question the addition of phenergan to pethidine for the woman in labour. First, only a very few women actually vomit or are nauseated following a minimal dose of pethidine. Second, phenergan appears to have an amnesic effect and, as women naturally remember their labours for years and years afterwards, there may be a need to be able to remember, and we may well be depriving women of something very important to them if we deprive them of this memory. Sparine added to pethidine has the same effect.

As I see it, the skills of the midwife are to help a woman feel so secure that she can surrender to the huge force taking over her body and to help her to 'ride' the periods of intense pain and panic by distracting her, by buying time, by supportive words and actions. For many women it is immensely important that they should manage to give birth without analgesia — not because they are masochists, but because they have carefully avoided drugs during pregnancy due to their known effect on the fetus and also because they want to protect their baby from drugs during labour.

Women who use no analgesia feel enormous pride that they have managed to overcome this overwhelmingly powerful feeling on their own. It seems to boost their confidence in themselves, and they feel capable of achieving anything. Often it confirms to them that being a mother is something they are uniquely cut out to be. It seems to me to be enormously important that we should help women to achieve a drug-free labour if this is what they want, especially as doing so is so dependent on the attitude of the midwife — it is she who really can make or break a woman's resolve to do without drugs.

Another skill of the midwife is to help a woman who has passionately wanted to do without drugs to come to terms with the fact that she needed some. When a woman has had only a small dose of pethidine (and this underlines how important this subject is to women, because women who have only had 50 mg of pethidine are usually just as upset as women who have had a much larger amount), I point out that in terms of strength of analgesia she has probably only taken four aspirins-worth and that, if she had had four aspirins, she probably would not be fretting about it at all.

When women have needed an epidural, I point out that all labours are different and that so much depends on the way the baby is lying. The long backache labour of a posterior-positioned baby is almost designed for the relief provided by an epidural, and the pain of syntocinon-induced contractions is much more intense and strong than pain from contractions that occur naturally. (Evidence for this comes from Sheila Kitzinger's study of 838 women who experienced induction of labour in the 1970s.) Sadly, even with all the counselling you are able to give, many women find it impossible to reconcile themselves to having had analgesia and they determine to 'do better next time' and to pursue a goal of 'perfection'. Perhaps this is to do with how we as women perceive ourselves, and probably in this case the midwife cannot help much. Nevertheless, because we were there and because we have so much influence on the use of analgesia in labour, we have to take responsibility for the distress of women when they have had analgesia which they wanted at the time but regret afterwards. Furthermore, as we were there, it is we who can remind them of how strong the labour was and of how they managed for hours without anything at all and of how they managed brilliantly with this or that part of their labour.

The difference between women and their desires for labour are eternally fascinating. I remember well two women I delivered five years ago, both on the same day, with the same student midwife. It was a Sunday. They were both multips. The first one was very glamorous and very neat, taking enormous trouble with her hair and makeup. She looked like a film star. She opted for an epidural and had a syntocinon drip, and I remember that as the baby's head emerged over the perineum she literally laughed the baby out. Each time she laughed, a little bit more of the baby's head emerged. It was a beautiful labour and delivery, enjoyed by her, by her husband and by me and the student. When that labour had finished and we were just about to transfer them all to the postnatal ward, the telephone in the labour ward rang. It was a woman who I had booked for a home delivery and who was now in labour. The student and I sped to the house which was on a council estate in my area.

During the hospital labour, the student midwife and I had

eaten chocolates supplied by the husband and drunk cups of tea supplied by us. At the home delivery, we ate sandwiches and drank cups of tea supplied by the husband. The baby was born after about four hours with no analgesia. It was a beautiful delivery and a very happy experience for us all — woman, husband, big brother (aged six), student midwife and me. In fact, the GP arrived soon after the delivery and made me giggle by asking me if I had 'been taking anything' because I was so 'high'. I reassured him that I had not, but that it had been my privilege to have been present in one day at both ends of the spectrum of obstetric care, and both had been wonderful and exciting.

One of the best analgesics for women in labour is to take a warm bath. This can be topped up frequently with warm water, and it is perfectly feasible to listen to the fetal heart with a Pinard's stethoscope if the woman lifts her abdomen up to you. The only danger is that the midwife often gets her hair damp!

As labour progresses the woman goes more and more inside herself. The best way to facilitate this is to keep the room in total darkness, devoid of any outside stimuli, but this is often impossible in modern labour wards. To counteract this, the woman can be encouraged to close her eyes or to lie with a damp dark flannel over them. Often she will do this spontaneously with no prompting from the midwife.

As the intensity of the contractions builds up and they become longer and closer together, the woman will naturally rotate her pelvis to encourage her baby into a position which is conducive to the rotation and flexion of the baby's head. Her feet will tense up at each contraction and assume extraordinary contortions as if the alternative pain of contorting the feet might help to distract the mind from the pain of the contractions.

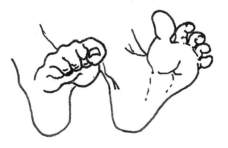

As the pain becomes harder, stronger and more intense, the woman approaches the 'transitional phase' of labour described by Grantley Dick Read and more recently by Erna Wright in *The New Childbirth*. She sometimes vomits or begins to tremble or feels like giving up. 'I want to go home *now*. I'll come back tomorrow and finish off.' 'I'm exhausted — all I want is a little sleep.' 'I want an epidural, general anaesthetic, anything.' Or perhaps more difficult than anything else — 'Help me, Caroline, please help me. *Do* something.' How can we resist? We who are trained for action? This is where we have to look at our own feelings and and needs and where we have to recognise our need to *do* something. I remember a midwife who was obviously feeling rather unsure of her sexual relationship with her new partner and who always gave women a massive dose of pethidine when they came to the end of the first stage of labour and began to make the throaty sensual noises that women make and many midwives love to hear. It seemed to me that she could not bear to hear that noise which for her had painful and disturbing connotations.

When a woman pleads with us to '*do* something', what can we do to help our own unease and discomfort? I often say 'We're here, we're with you. You are all right. It's meant to feel like this. You are doing well. The reason it's so painful is because it's progressing quickly. Everything is fine, you're doing wonderfully. You are so clever, you look so good, you are so relaxed. Brilliant, brilliant. Keep going, it's not long now'. When a woman says to me 'I can't cope with any more', I say — 'But you are coping. You are coping beautifully. You will never be sent more than you can cope with, and soon it will be over and the baby will be here. Come on, you are doing so well'.

Sometimes at these moments of stress, it helps to get the woman to come out of herself and look into your eyes during a contraction. The sensation is extraordinary because you can feel the strength being sucked out of you into her. It often makes me want to cry but I firmly resist the feeling because I do not think it would be helpful to the woman if I were to weep all over her!

If the woman begins to cry, I firmly but gently tell her 'Come on Georgina. You're getting on so well. Don't give up now that you're so near'. This is usually enough to help women to regain their feelings of control and of being able to manage. In the cold light of reason, the woman has nothing to cry about. She is having a baby, something that many women long to do but never manage. She is coming to the end of a long pregnancy and labour, and relief is nearly at hand. Another thought is that this is only 24 hours out of her whole life. These thoughts might strike you as being rather hard, but I believe that for the woman to keep her strength up she cannot be allowed to wallow in self-pity. It is not at all helpful and can drag her down.

Labour is an endurance test and there are several ways to increase a woman's pain threshold.

1. Distraction such as a bath, watching a video or television, going for a walk or playing cards.
2. Keeping the head above the uterus (keep your chin up).
3. Knowing at all times what is happening.
4. Releasing endorphins by going inside herself.
5. Being at a comfortable temperature.
6. Eating little snacks and drinking pleasant, fresh tasting fruit juices or herb teas. This keeps up the blood sugar levels and is also a distraction.

As labour draws towards the second stage, an extraordinary change takes place. The woman relaxes and often dozes off to sleep between contractions. The contractions slow down to allow this 'rest and be thankful' phase to occur. Often this quiet patch can take up an hour or more. She will wake up when the contractions build up again. Then the woman can no longer keep her knees together and they have to be apart. This obviously increases the pelvic diameters, and she will rotate her pelvis if she has room and is not confined on a narrow, hard bed. She will often pass a 'bloody show', a large plug of mucus coloured with fresh blood, and she will increasingly moan and make deep throaty noises like the ones women make during sexual intercourse.

As the baby's head descends down the vagina, the woman gyrates as her discomfort increases and as the extraordinary feeling of the baby's head descending fills her consciousness. Her vulva and her anus begin to bulge around the baby's head, and soon a catch comes into her breathing as she quite involuntarily begins to push the baby out. For some women this feeling is so enormous that it feels as though their whole body has been taken over by some huge force. It can be as uncontrollable as vomiting.

It is hardly ever necessary to tell a woman to push. She always knows when and how to push her baby out, unless we have encouraged her to push too early when the baby is still up high in her vagina. In the modern labour ward the great worry during the second stage is always the activity of the fetal heart. When this is continuously monitored, it always dips alarmingly during the second stage. It is probably better, therefore, for everyone's peace of mind to use a sonic aid between each contraction when the fetal heart will be heard to have regained its previous speed and variability.

DELIVERY POSITIONS

A woman can deliver in a variety of positions. She can stand up and cling to her partner with the midwife kneeling on the floor behind the woman ready to 'catch' the baby. Alternatively, the woman can take up the same standing position but with her partner behind her and supporting her. The midwife has a slightly better view with the woman this way round.

A very comfortable way for women to deliver is on all fours, either leaning on a bean bag or just supporting herself. The midwife can kneel behind her to deliver the baby. The view for the midwife is excellent but it is rather awkward for the midwife to have to 'post' the baby up towards the mother's head end. It

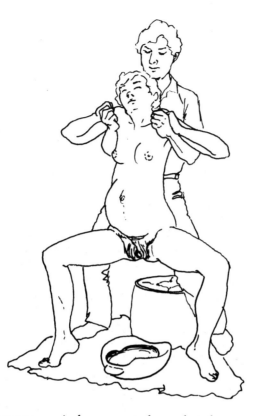

is important to remind women to keep their knees as wide apart as possible to ensure a wide pelvis during delivery in this position.

Bean bags are very comfortable to deliver on as long as the woman's coccyx has freedom to extend backwards. Some women choose to deliver on a bed, of course, and they too need to be off their coccyx. This can be achieved with pillows under their back or with the woman in the left (or right) lateral position with her leg supported by her partner or with a stool (See Chapter Six).

Few women need an episiotomy if the midwife is patient and allows the woman to push at her own pace. The perineum thins out and usually the baby's head gently emerges over the perineum leaving it intact or with only a slight graze or nick. The motto for episiotomies should always be — 'Wait, now wait a little longer, now wait some more'.

When a baby comes out, it usually takes a few seconds to begin spontaneous respiration. Leaving the still pulsating cord alone and uncut will ensure that the baby is getting some oxygen. Gentle and firm massaging of the baby will encourage it to start breathing and will give you something to do to assuage your anxiety until the baby does start breathing regularly on its own. A few babies need gentle sucking out with a mucus extractor, but this must be done with great gentleness to avoid vagal nerve stimulation and spasm. Another gentle way of removing mucus from a baby's mouth and throat is to lie the baby face down on your knees and to gently elevate the feet end of the baby while gently stroking and massaging the baby's

chest. In fact most babies who have not had any analgesia begin to breathe as soon as their heads emerge from their mother's body. If the woman is in an upright position, the mucus flows out from the baby's nose and mouth as the chest is squeezed in the vagina.

In most hospitals midwives are encouraged to give an injection of syntometrine as the baby emerges, but this can have repercussions for the mother which may not be entirely welcome. Sally Inch points out in her brilliant book *Birthrights* that the sequelae of an injection of syntometrine can be headache, dizziness, ringing in the ears, chest pain, palpitations, cramp in the back and legs and a rise in blood pressure. These symptoms may or may not occur, but a certain and very unpleasant result of the routine administration of syntometrine is the 'unholy rush' which then ensues in order to get the placenta delivered before the cervix closes and traps it. To avoid this disgusting haste, which disturbs all that is going on between the parents and the baby, it is often helpful to leave the cord until it has stopped pulsating — which will take up to 30 minutes — and then give the syntometrine and deliver the placenta by controlled cord traction about three minutes later. In fact in about half the women you are looking after, the placenta will already have come away spontaneously.

Birth is remembered by the woman for ever. It colours her feelings about herself, about her baby and about the rest of her family. Nowadays women only have one or two children. If they have a devastating experience of birth, it will affect most of their life. Giving birth can be an ecstatic and miraculous experience for a woman, but it can also be a nightmare. So much depends on the midwife, who can make even a long and unpleasant labour bearable by her encouragement and caring.

- Good.
- Excellent.
- You're doing so well.
- You're beautifully relaxed.
- Let it happen.
- Let it come.
- Let it open you up.
- Surrender to it.
- Feel yourself opening up.
- Good.
- Good.
- Good.
- Well done.
- That's wonderful.
- That's marvellous.
- Oh how brilliant.
- That's lovely.
- Blossom.
- Flourish.
- Open up to it.
- Be soft.
- Be giving.
- Surrender to it.
- Give, give, give.
- Surrender.
- Open, open.
- Good.
- Good, Good.

References and Further Reading

Dick Read, G. (1956). *Childbirth Without Fear*. London: William Heinemann Medical Books Ltd.
Inch, S. (1982). *Birthrights*. London: Hutchinson Ltd.

Kitzinger, S. (1975 and 1978). *Some Mothers' Experiences of Induced Labour. Submission to the Department of Health & Social Security from the National Childbirth Trust.* London: National Childbirth Trust.

Klein, M., Lloyd, I., Redman, C., Bull, M., Turnbull, A. C. (1983). A comparison of low-risk women booked for delivery in two systems of care: shared-care (consultant) and integrated general practice unit. I. Obstetrical procedures and neonatal outcome. II. Labour and delivery management and neonatal outcome. *British Journal of Obstetrics and Gynaecology*; Vol. 90: 118–22 and 123–8 (February).

Wright, E. (1964). *The New Childbirth.* Tandem.

Chapter Five

Labour Partner

Probably the most important role for any partner of a woman in labour is just to *be there*. Just having someone who is there, caring about her and only her, is a great comfort. This still applies even if the midwife is the dearest and most trusted of friends, because her role is always to be caring about the health of the mother and baby and as such she will be taking a more detached view than a partner.

The conversation of the partner needs to be directed to the woman in labour. It is always very tempting for the midwife or the medical attendants to chat to the husband but this should be avoided. Birth is not a social event. It is a huge life-changing experience for the woman and as such should be respected. Idle gossip has no place in the labour ward — it is a place in which miracles take place, and behaviour in the labour ward or the room where labour is taking place should be full of the respect a happening as momentous as this should command.

Apart from concentrating on the woman, partners can help in other ways, and the wise midwife will make sure that the partner feels part of the whole process and not in the way or useless. Life is made so much easier for midwives when the woman has someone with her, and we can do a great deal to help the partner to enjoy the day as well. Labour demands so much of modern men. It is a frightening and isolating position for them. Compare labour today — which takes place in an alienating and strange environment, with the couple on their own, the man experiencing his first labour too — with a more primitive or traditional situation in which the woman is surrounded by women supporting her. In the more traditional situation, many of these women would be experienced in births and would be excited rather than nervous. For the modern man, all alone at a labour, it is extremely stressful and he needs help, guidance and support from the midwife. If the partners are women, the atmosphere is different, especially if they are women who have borne children — they are much more confident about the process. The atmosphere is different again if the husband comes with the woman's mother or sister, or with one of his female relatives.

To start off and to enable the man to feel at ease and useful, he can be encouraged to do practical things during the labour. He can pour tea, fetch iced water, go to the shop for sweets and newspapers, take his wife to the shop for sweets and newspapers. He can be a companion to the woman when she is in the bath, on the lavatory, going for a walk round the hospital or when the midwife has to nip out to fetch a VE trolley or to find a monitor. During the intense part of labour, he can act as a slave who provides instant cold flannels for the face, the back of the neck, the back or the chest, and instant sips of water between frequent contractions.

The sensitive partner can also be there to be grumbled at and the butt of snappy remarks which could not be made to anyone else. He can also be a soul mate against the over enthusiastic midwife — 'Well, it's all very well for her, bouncing about, but it's bloody agony for me.'

A partner can be frightened by the unusual and throaty noises a woman may make at the end of the first stage of labour. The reassuring words 'It's all right, Joan. This is how it's meant to be. It's all right. It's meant to feel like that', and to the father, 'She's getting on ever so well — really surrendering to the sensations', will reassure both of them.

Partners can be an immense support when labour is getting really hard. I remember with great amusement a woman who had always said that she did not want any analgesia and who, when labour was getting hard, said to me 'Caroline, I've changed my mind. I want an epidural', only to be countered by her two women friends, who said firmly, 'Oh no, Joyce, you want natural childbirth' and who firmly deflected her from having an epidural throughout her labour. They took her for 'a little walk' each time she came near to voicing her wishes for an epidural and, after it was all over, she turned to these two very tough ladies with a radiant smile as she cradled her new-born son and said, 'Oh thank you both so much. I nearly didn't manage, but I'm so glad I did'.

I also think with great admiration of the mother of a rather immature 18 year old who cherished her daughter through labour, telling her quite firmly at the beginning that she was not going to need anything, but that Mum would be here all the time. Mum was there all the time, and daughter did not need anything except for a couple of whiffs of Entonox just before second stage while her legs were being put up in stirrups, as her baby was presenting by the breech and was about to be delivered by an obstetrician.

So often it is the support of people around the woman in labour that helps her through it. The midwife can be of inestimable help by helping to keep the spirits up of everyone in the room. I recall a woman in labour who had with her not only her husband, but also a couple they were very friendly with and their toddler son. The little boy ran around the labour ward and the bathroom (where she spent a total of seven hours in the bath) and played and helped 'wash' the labouring woman by splashing the bath water at her. Both couples spent a long time chatting together, only stopping for each contraction. I think that the number of people in the room probably made the labour rather longer than it might otherwise have been, but little Thomas certainly acted as a good distraction and the new mother was adamant afterwards that she could not have managed without the help of her friends. She was a primigravida and she laboured for about 12 hours without any analgesia at all. She delivered on a bean bag and sustained no perineal trauma. Her baby emerged with an Apgar score of nine at one minute and ten at five minutes, and since that excellent start in life she has been breastfed and has thrived.

The presence of friends can make everything more normal and home-like, and can help the woman to feel relaxed and secure. Each time I deliver a woman at home, I realise how very different the atmosphere is from that in the hospital. However hard we try to make the hospital more like a home, and I have to admit that sadly the will to achieve this is not very strong, the hospital is basically very different from a home and probably the two can never be truly alike.

At home the room belongs to the woman and her partner. In hospital there is no privacy and many rooms have grilles on the door so that faces or just an eye peer in — like a prison cell. I have never yet encountered a delivery room in hospital where the door can be locked. Not that one would need to lock a room at home, but at home strangers would not keep coming in to 'borrow a sphyg' or 'just to fill your shelves'. The lack of privacy in modern labour wards increases the stress for the woman, her partner and the midwife. The woman would probably prefer to be in darkness, somewhere completely private and secure. With the lack of privacy in modern labour wards, she has no security. Just as she withdraws inside herself, someone flings open the door and comes in — sometimes 'just to borrow a sphyg', sometimes to enquire if she needs the anaesthetist 'who is here at the moment'. Sometimes it is a doctor, asking how everything is going. The father is aware of all the comings and goings. It keeps him alert and he may quite enjoy the distraction. But he will also be aware that it is harming the atmosphere in the room, especially if the group is ever left alone long enough for the peaceful atmosphere conducive to progress in labour to develop.

Sheila Kitzinger's analogy of the modern labour ward in her book *Woman's Experience of Sex* is too incisive and perceptive to miss. 'It is as if we were required to make love, pouring ourselves, body and mind, into the full expression of feeling, in a busy airport concourse, a large railway terminus, in a gymnasium or a tiled public lavatory.'

For the midwife the constant interruptions are a bugbear. They stop her from being able to help the woman into the deep introspection of labour. Often the midwife has to justify her practice. 'Why haven't you ruptured the membranes?' 'When are you doing the next vaginal examination?' 'Why aren't you using a monitor?' I have found that one of the ways to counter this barrage of questions is actually to be in physical contact with the woman when a doctor comes into the labour ward, to have your hand on the woman's abdomen, feeling contractions. This may in fact be very aggravating for the woman, but it seems to subdue doctors in the same way that having a roomful of female relatives and friends in the delivery room or having the woman in the bath does.

I work with many doctors whom I love and respect. I have learnt a great deal from some of them, but I think we need to bear in mind what is happening in the modern labour ward. Doctors are overproducing. There are too many for our needs. Think about what is happening if you work in a unit in which 2000 women are delivered a year. Most midwives and obstetricians would agree that about 80% of pregnant women could deliver without medical aid. Therefore, of these 2000 women, 1600 could deliver without any aid except for the midwife's encouragement. This means that 400 women a year will need help from the doctors. That is actually just over seven women a week — one woman a day needing help out of the 40 labouring women going through that labour ward a week. This means that if doctors do not intervene in a huge number of labours, there just is not enough for the medical staff to do.

Nobody deliberately intervenes in a labour which is progressing well, but women are in such a suggestive state during labour that it is very easy to interfere with the normal progress of that labour. By never allowing the woman to 'settle' in her labour, by providing constant interruptions which distract the woman and make her anxious, by having a high anxiety level in the labour ward, the labour can become prolonged so that it becomes 'necessary' to intervene.

The other factor that we need to realise is that only a very few doctors working in obstetrics at the moment have ever seen a normal labour and delivery from beginning to end. Most medical students have only spent approximately seven days in a labour ward during their training. During these brief seven days, they will have been called to see any complication which is happening while they are there. 'Quick, Mark, there's a breech in Room 5.' 'Jane, do you want to see twins delivered?' 'Joseph, there's a caesarean in a minute.'

During their time as students, it is almost impossible for the embryonic doctors to be present from the beginning to the end of a labour. If they do manage to do so, it will be for only one or two. Once the doctor has qualified, he or she becomes a house officer and, if working on the labour ward, is the person to whom midwives have to report any abnormalities. Now remember, this doctor is someone who during his or her training spent seven days in an environment in which the midwife has often spent years. The house officer spends six months in this position and then becomes a registrar, doing forceps deliveries, caesareans, ventouse deliveries, fetal blood sampling and perceiving him or herself as the guide and director of the midwives.

It is easy to see then, when you look at medical training, that most doctors working in obstetrics today really have no inkling of what a normal labour is. They are excellent at dealing with a crisis. They are wizard at performing a caesarean. If a woman is going to have a labour which does not run normally, the doctors who take care of her during this time are probably safer and more expert at dealing with abnormalities than doctors at any other time in our history. We must recognise, however, that this is their expertise and that normal labour is a closed book as far as they are concerned. It is midwives who know about normal labour and who have a responsibility to women to guard it.

If someone only knows about one aspect of childbirth (that is that it can go wrong, and be abnormal), if all the labours that a person sees are like that (because that is why they are there), and if they do not know about the 70–80% of labours which progress normally (without interference), they will rush in with syntocinon during the 'rest and be thankful' phase at the end of the first stage of labour because they will think of it as 'delay in first stage' or 'uterine inertia'. And they will suggest that a woman starts pushing because she is fully dilated, even though the head has not descended enough for her to have a pushing urge yet.

It is up to the midwife, who has seen normal labours progressing through their slow leisurely stages to defuse the situation, to deflect and dissuade the doctor, to sit beside the woman, holding her hand, with her hand on her abdomen or in some way in physical connection with her — being 'with' her. 'Joan's feeling fine. She's really doing well. She doesn't want a drip at this stage, but she may be open to having one in an hour and a half or two hours' time.' 'Yes, she is fully dilated, but she has no urge to push yet, and she doesn't want to waste her energy until she really has an overwhelming urge.' These things are easy to say here but are often very difficult to say at the time. But remember the knowledge that you have. It is difficult for us to acknowledge how much we know. We need a support group to help with that, and a birth register of our own to tot up the number of labours we have been at and what we have learnt from each one. It is always difficult for us as women to praise and admire ourselves but it is very important that we do so, not just for our own sakes, but for the women we care for.

Partners in Labour — What are the Basics for Them?

• To be there — with the woman — someone on her side.

- To respond to her needs — a cool flannel, a drink.
- To encourage — that's right, you're doing beautifully.
- To compliment — you look so beautiful, so lovely.
- To massage and knead — her back, her feet.
- To stroke — her legs, her tummy, her back (very light featherlike strokes).
- To kiss — her neck, her mouth, her back, her thighs, especially if the atmosphere becomes strained. It will bring normality into the situation.
- To communicate — Emily has always said that she wanted to deliver on the birth chair.
- To repeat — the midwife says she can see the baby's hair.
- To remind — don't forget, they said in the classes that forceps only take about five minutes from start to finish. Don't forget they said that the transition was the time you might feel like giving up. Don't forget, it's a baby, it'll be here soon.

For the partner, labour is long and gruelling, but it is also one of life's peak experiences, something he will never forget, something which will help him to understand his partner better and women in general better.

After the birth, the partner has perhaps an even more important role. He must encourage his partner to talk through the labour with him. Labour needs to be talked through time and time again. This is healing and cathartic for both the partners. One of them will remember things that the other does not. They also need to talk it through with the midwife who was with them. This is a primary function of ours which we do not often think of and do not allow time for.

It is even more important for the midwife to talk through the birth of a baby when the woman has had a caesarean under general anaesthetic. The midwife needs to be able to take the woman step by step through the operation, to describe exactly what the baby looked like (reinforced by photographs), what the baby did — whimper, cry loudly, look very pale and still, do a wee, move its arms — what was done to the baby, who held it, how the baby was resuscitated, how the baby responded. When the baby first met its father, how the father looked, what the father said, how the baby looked. When the baby first met its mother, what the baby did, how the mother lay, what she said. All of this should, if possible, be reinforced by photographs.

The partner and the midwife are really there for the same thing — to be with the woman during her childbirth and to support and cherish her. Perhaps the midwife also needs to cherish the partner as well.

I remember with gratitude a man who was sitting alone and crying in a delivery room several years ago. I just had to go in and put my arms around him and cherish him. I did not know what had happened to him or his wife because I was just passing through, but his need was so obvious that I responded. It turned out that his wife had been taken off to have an emergency caesarean under general anaesthetic. While I was with him and holding him, his baby was brought out to him. We both examined the baby and rejoiced at this little person. I said goodbye when he was finally reunited with his wife.

I had forgotten all about this incident until last year when a man who looked vaguely familiar sought me out and said — 'I've been looking all over for you. We're having another baby tomorrow. It's going to be an epidural caesarean this time. Little Timothy is four now. You don't remember who I am, do you? I'm the man . . .'.

I expressed gratitude to this man at the beginning of this story. This is why — it was a day when I felt very down, very ineffectual, when all my dreams had apparently come to an end, when I was wondering whether to creep away and retire to write radio plays and bake cakes. This man came and reinforced my self-image. He came to say thank you and to show me that I had done something that mattered at a time of great need.

This is the great joy of being a midwife — the fact that you are carried in people's hearts and minds forever, are forever associated with a tremendously powerful event. We take part in a miracle every day. We are loved, beloved and cherished. We are privy to an experience of such intimacy that we shall never experience anything remotely approaching it unless we live in a very close sexual relationship with another person. Midwife — with woman, with people, with babies, with parents, with joy, with love.

Chapter Six

Delivery in Different Positions

Delivering women in different positions is not difficult, but it often helps to see pictures of the way the baby will be coming out so that when you first perform a delivery in an unaccustomed position, you will not be shocked or frightened. Many midwives say that when women are left to their own devices they are mobile during the first stage of labour but always end up by delivering on a bed. I am not at all sure about this because my own experience is very different. I find that women, when given a choice between bed, bean bag with soft mat, birth chair or standing up, nearly always seem to plump for kneeling on all fours resting on the bean bag with their knees on the mat. Delivering on the birth chair comes second. This is when they have a real choice and all these alternatives are there ready and available and dotted around the room.

The important factor when a woman is in labour is not where she finally delivers. It is the ability to move around restlessly during labour.

Labour is painful. The pain is a deep throbbing, a hot vibrating ache deep inside the woman's body. Labour is powerful. The strength of it fills her whole being, takes her over, engulfs her. It is not comfortable and, with the combination of the painfulness and the enormous power, a woman frequently wants and needs to move around, gyrate and stagger from table to worktop to armchair.

As Janet and Arthur Balaskas say in *Active Birth Manifesto*, 'In every uninhibited labour, there is a marked restlessness: the woman walks, stands, squats, kneels, lies down and moves her body freely to find the most comfortable and appropriate positions. There can be no fixed position for a natural healthy labour and birth when a woman follows her own instincts — for birth is active, involving a succession of changing positions, and is not a passive "confinement"'.

At home it is easy to be restless, to lean against this surface

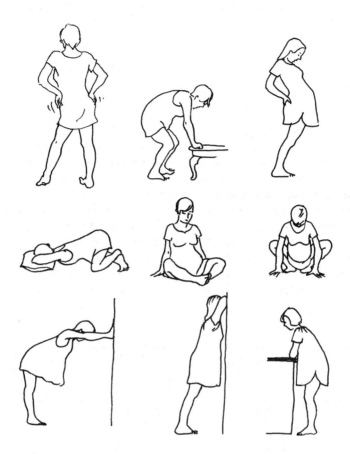

during this contraction, against this wall for the next, to kneel forward onto the settee for the next. Home has a variety of surfaces and furniture that it is impossible to replicate in a hospital.

Another advantage of home is that it is private. At home the woman, whose naked bottom is on view during a contraction (because she has decided to adopt the knee chest position because it seems comfortable for the next 30 seconds), does not mind exposing her bottom to the assembled company because usually there are only a very few people, whom she has chosen to be with her. The same situation in hospital, even when the woman has a midwife she knows and loves, is lacking in privacy because at any moment the door may be flung open and someone will come in. These interruptions are intolerable and hopefully we shall one day realise this.

Yet another great help for an active labour is to remove as many stimuli as possible, so that the woman can go deep inside herself and open up to the enormous feelings inside her. As Michel Odent says, she reaches a different plane of consciousness and releases endorphins which help her overcome the pain. The midwife, the guardian of normal labour, has enormous influence on the woman's labour. It is she who can protect the woman from visitors coming into the room uninvited. It is she who encourages the woman. It is she who believes that this woman's body will work — because she has seen the process work a hundred times before and she knows deep in her psyche that women's bodies work, that the baby will come unaided from this woman's body, that the woman will manage.

It is she alone who enables the woman to be free during her labour, enables her to take up any position she finds comfortable. The midwife can leave the room as it always is, with the

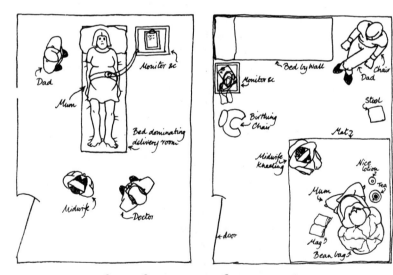

A Conventional Delivery Room.   Better use of the same space.

bed taking up the whole room so that, although the woman is determined to be active and mobile during labour, she ends up on the bed because there just is not anywhere else for her to be.

The labour ward can be all bed, or it can be a room which has a bed in it along with other furniture, like a chair or a bean bag, or even just a mat. If the bed is pushed against the wall, so that the woman can get onto it if she wants to and the midwife can stand at the side if she needs to, it will release more floor space for the woman to be active in.

Having ensured that the woman you are with has freedom to move and has real choice about what position she decides to take up, the next step for the midwife is to be aware of how the baby will be coming out.

To be aware of how the baby is lying and to accustom yourself to the way in which the baby will come out when a woman is in a different position from the standard one, you need to think of the way the baby is lying in the position you are used to and then translate it to another position. This is not always easy but can be learnt with practice.

It is important for midwives to get to know the feel of babies' heads very well. When you are washing babies or changing their nappies, gently feel their heads and identify the posterior fontanelle and the lambdoidal suture. Run your fingers along the sagittal suture. Feel the occiput and the two parietal bones.

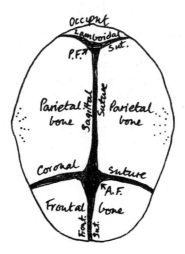

Get to know the feel of a baby's head so well that when you feel something on vaginal examination, you will almost instantly be able to recognise it.

If you palpate the woman's abdomen first, before performing a vaginal examination, hopefully you will know what position you think the baby is lying in. Then you can try to equate the position you are feeling on vaginal examination with how the baby is lying in the uterus.

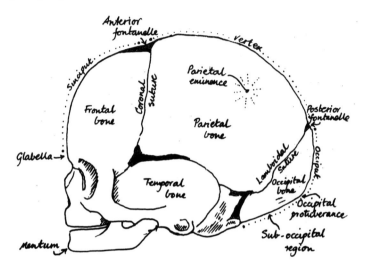

With posterior positioned babies, the woman experiences backache, the labour is usually slower, and the contractions less effective because the baby's head is deflexed. (Flexion means bent. For example, the baby is so curled up at the latter part of the first stage of labour that she normally has her chin on her chest.) When the baby's head is deflexed, a larger area of the baby's head comes first (the suboccipito-frontal diameter which is 10 cm compared with the suboccipito-bregmatic diameter which is 9·5 cm), the head does not fit into the lower segment of the uterus so snugly, the cervix is not so well stimulated and contractions are not so effective.

In this next illustration of what you will feel when the baby is lying in a right occipito-posterior position, the lambdoidal suture and posterior fontanelle are easily recognisable. The head might well be more deflexed and then you would be able to feel more of the sagittal suture and some of the anterior fontanelle. The sagittal suture is in the right oblique diameter of the pelvis which it would also be if the head were lying in the LOA position.

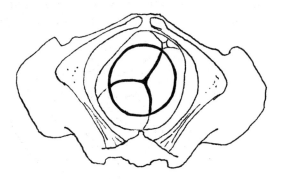

ROP Prone

A skill of ancient midwives was always to try to encourage the deflexed head to flex more and to encourage rotation into an anterior position manually when the woman had reached second stage.

In the *Family Medicine Reporter* of September 1977, Dr Charles H. Wright describes a technique he has explored for rotating the baby's head into an anterior position. He would press up on the anterior fontanelle so as to flex the baby's head. Then because 'the head is smooth and covered with vernix, so you can't turn it with your finger alone. You must be sure to anchor your fingernail in the crease between the bones (the lambdoidal suture). And do it during a contraction; otherwise the head won't turn easily.'

'The idea is to bring the posterior fontanelle forward from the 3, 6 or 9 o'clock position. Then the baby is more deliverable. In the right-sided position you rotate it clockwise. In the left-sided position you should rotate it counterclockwise.'

It also makes sense that this technique would be easier if the woman were kneeling on all fours as it would bring the baby off the mother's spine. If you rotate the picture above, you will see how the vaginal examination feels when it has been performed with the woman on her hands and knees.

Doing a vaginal examination with the woman standing up (if

that is the most comfortable position for her) is excellent for the midwife because it is very easy to feel the landmarks, especially if the woman comes down onto your fingers so that you can feel a posterior cervix easily.

The landmarks are the same as when the woman is lying down, as you can see from this drawing of the LOA position.

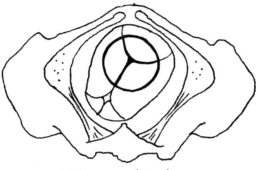

LOA prone and standing

If a woman is most comfortable on her left side, the landmarks of the fetal head will appear like this on vaginal examination. The baby here is also lying in a left occipito- anterior position.

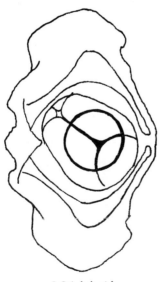

LOA left side

If the woman is on all fours, the landmarks when the baby is in a left occipito-anterior position are —

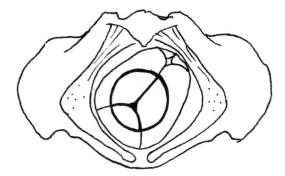

LOA on all fours

Delivering a baby in the left lateral position is very easy. You have a great deal of control over the baby's head to stop it emerging very quickly. You can put warm pads on the perineum. In the next drawing, the woman is holding her own legs, but often her partner can do that or she can rest her leg on the midwife's shoulders although that is very heavy for the midwife.

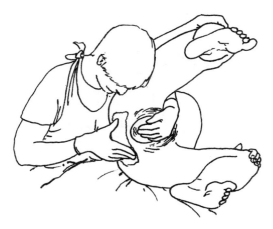

I would never have anticipated asking for a drawing of a woman delivering in the right lateral until that was the position a woman took up about a year ago. She found it the only possible position. I found it very awkward but if I had seen this next picture beforehand I would have felt more prepared. As you can see, she put her leg on a small stool which she found supported it comfortably.

When a woman squats, delivering her is the same as when she is lying in a dorsal position except it is easier because her legs do not get in the way so much.

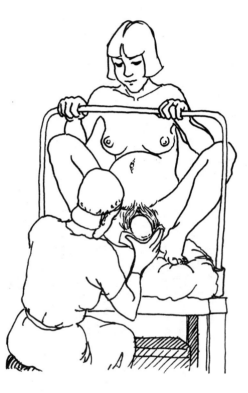

On a birthchair it is also easy to deliver. The baby comes out in the same way as it does when the woman is in a dorsal position. It is not so easy to see the perineum, and the midwife needs to have a soft mat to sit on. It is a lovely position for the woman, who can put her hand down and feel the baby's head and help to deliver the baby if she wants to. Notice the bedpan underneath to catch drips and to give an accurate assessment of blood loss. In fact, many people believe that a woman bleeds more when she uses a birthchair. It may well be that the measurement is simply more accurate.

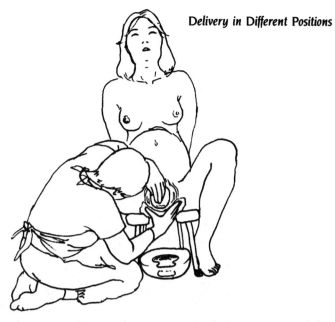

In the next picture the woman is being supported by her partner, who is sitting on a low stool. She is sitting on a bedpan which can be extremely comfortable if it is well designed. It also catches any blood and amniotic fluid.

As I have said, I find that the majority of women seem to prefer to be delivered in the all fours position. It is a wonderful position for the midwife. She has a marvellous view of the perineum and the advancing baby's head, and it is easy to deliver the baby slowly and smoothly. Once the head is out (and remember the baby in the above drawing is looking at the midwife, his face would be under her left hand), the mucus streams out of the baby's nose and mouth. Babies born in this position rarely need any mucus extraction. The only awkward part of this position is that, after delivering the anterior and then the posterior shoulder, the baby is then taken up towards the mother so that she can enfold him when she is ready. Often it is a good idea just to lie the baby on the floor underneath her breast and face, and then she can pick him up. This is quite an awkward manoeuvre — I feel that I am 'posting' the baby up to its mother!

Giving women the opportunity to deliver in whichever way they are most happy makes delivering babies even more exciting. It is never the same any two days running. Everyone chooses something slightly different. Each labour is an adventure and a tremendous learning experience. And it helps to make us midwives more agile, which cannot be bad.

References and Further Reading

Balaskas, A., Balaskas, J. (1983). *Active Birth Manifesto*. London: Active Birth Movement. (See Appendix 5 for address.)

Family Medicine Reporter (1977). Report on manual rotation to shorten prolonged labour. September issue.

Odent, M. (1984). *Birth Reborn*. New York: Random House Inc.

Chapter Seven

Monitoring in Different Positions

First of all, we need to look at what we are monitoring and why we are monitoring. We are monitoring (checking and being aware of) changes in the health and physical and emotional well-being of the mother, and we are monitoring (checking and being aware of) the condition of the baby. These things we do in many ways. We sit quietly and just absorb the atmosphere of the woman, murmuring the odd supportive word where appropriate but mostly leaving her to get on with her labour. We check her pulse from time to time. We check her blood pressure as necessary (aware that this is a very disturbing action on our part, which interrupts the flow of the labour). We test her urine, and we take her temperature occasionally.

We generally keep aware of how she is. We check for cervical dilatation occasionally but again we are aware that this can be very disturbing for a woman as we are going against the whole flow of her body. In times gone by, midwives felt that it was unnecessary to perform vaginal examinations because they could tell how far a woman was on in labour just by looking at her. I learnt this from the midwife who delivered my first baby and from whom I learnt what I as a mother needed from a midwife. She was an old midwife. She could not hear very well so she did not listen to my son's heartbeat. I am amazed to say that this did not worry me in the least — her pleasure at being there with me and her supreme confidence in my ability to give birth were enough to instill supreme confidence in me. My lovely midwife also did not do vaginal examinations. Why should she need to? She had palpated my abdomen. She knew that the baby's head was engaged and was descending. She could look at me and see how I was coping and being and that was enough for her to know how far on I was.

We monitor the baby in two ways. We listen to her

heartbeat for regularity and speed, and we are aware of the
liquor if the membranes have ruptured. If they are clear or
pink (blood stained) and smell normal, we are happy. If they
are khaki (stale meconium stained), we are alert and aware
that the baby has been stressed during the previous few days.
If they are bright green, we are aware that the baby is passing
meconium during this labour and that we need to keep a much
closer eye on her heartbeat. At this time a scalp clip is
appropriate.

When the membranes have not ruptured and you are
listening to the baby's hearbeat with a Pinard's stethescope,
how accurate is it? How meaningful? How effective?

For two years, from 1981 to 1983, a study was carried out
at the National Maternity Hospital in Dublin on two groups
of women. In the first group, 6474 were continuously monitored with a fetal scalp clip attached to the baby's head and to
an electronic fetal monitor. In the other group, 6490 women
had intermittent auscultation, with the midwife listening to the
baby's heartbeat for 60 seconds at least every 15 minutes
during the first stage of labour and between every contraction
in the second stage of labour. If the heartbeat was difficult to
hear at any time, intermittent Doppler ultrasound was used.
What did the research show at the end? Did it show that the
babies who were monitored with an electronic fetal monitor
benefitted from it?

In both groups 14 babies died. The deaths of three in the
electronic fetal monitoring group were ascribed to traumatic
intracranial hemorrhage following forceps delivery. Furthermore the babies in the electronic fetal monitoring group were
33% more likely to be delivered by forceps than the babies in
the intermittent auscultation group. The rate of caesarean
section was the same in both groups. (This particular finding
differs from the results of other randomised studies which have
shown an increase in caesarean section with electronic fetal
monitoring.)

The Apgar scores of the babies were the same in both
groups, and so were the rates of admission to the special care
baby unit. The big difference was in the rate of neonatal
convulsions occurring in babies who were intermittently
auscultated. There were 39 babies who had convulsions in the
first year of their life — 27 of them were in the group which

had intermittent auscultation compared with 12 who were in the continuous electronic fetal monitoring group. At the end of a year, however, when the babies were examined, the same number in each group, three, were found to have severe disabilities. Neonatal convulsions were associated with longer labours and, strangely, women in this trial who were electronically monitored had quicker labours than women who were auscultated.

As the author, Adrian Grant, points out from this study, to prevent one case of neonatal convulsions which may or may not be important, it is necessary to monitor continuously 433 fetuses. But this figure may be as low as 240 or as high as 2167 fetuses monitored per case of neonatal convulsions. This means that in the mid-1980s, when most midwives average 23 deliveries per year, we are talking about each midwife monitoring all the women she delivers over the next ten years to prevent one case of neonatal convulsions or, at the other extreme, it could be that she has to monitor every woman she delivers for the next 94 years before she prevents one case of neonatal convulsions.

So it would seem that the results of research into the management of labour are really not conclusive. There are risks in being electronically monitored in that forceps deliveries are more common. There are risks in being auscultated in that neonatal convulsions are more common. There are risks in having a baby in hospital. There are risks in having a baby at home. There are risks in being human. It would seem that the decision to use electronic fetal monitoring should be made at the time and should be made with discretion. It can be useful and appropriate. It can also be a nuisance and very inappropriate.

There are two great disadvantages of continuous monitoring which may or may not be worth putting up with — and these need to be discussed with the parents.

The first great inconvenience is the very fact that the heartbeat is visible *all* the time. This, of course, is seen by some people as the great advantage of this type of monitoring, but it is very much a two-edged sword. First it is fascinating. It is like the screen of a computer, like the television on in the corner. You try not to watch it all the time but it exerts a hypnotic influence over almost everyone. In many labour wards, all over the country and at this very moment, there are small groups of people sitting hunched around fetal monitors watching with trance-like fascination the marker scratching away.

Being able to see the baby's heartbeat *all* the time means that we see every flicker, every change, every variation. Because we anxiously watch these, the anxiety level inside the room is heightened. The easiest way to interfere with the normal progress of labour, which is after all a normal physiological process, is to raise the anxiety level and so stop the woman from surrendering herself to the overwhelming sensations of her labour.

Earlier studies invariably show an increase in caesarean sections when routine continuous electronic fetal monitoring is carried out. Indeed in units where electronic fetal monitoring is used routinely, the caesarean section rate usually veers above the national average of 11%.

Being able to watch every nuance of the fetal heart means that we tend to react to every change. Everyone's heartbeat slows down or speeds up from time to time. I could almost guarantee that if a group of supposedly healthy people had a monitor on their hearts for the next 24 hours, someone would be able to find an abnormality or a worrying trend in several of them.

So having the baby's heartbeat printed out continuously means that we over-react. It also means that we tend to take our attention away from the woman and that we have a higher level of anxiety inside the labour room.

Another great disadvantage of monitoring is the way it tethers a woman down. With the help and encouragement of a willing midwife, a woman can be fairly mobile with a monitor attached, but usually it restricts her movements enormously. I have already quoted Arthur and Janet Balaskas's very descriptive paragraph from *Active Birth Manifesto* — 'In every labour there is a marked restlessness: the woman walks, stands, squats, kneels, lies down, and moves her body freely to find the most comfortable and appropriate positions'. Monitoring often confines this restlessness.

Caldeyro-Barcia, in his description of 'humanised labour' says that 'the mother should be free to select the position in which she feels more comfortable during labour, and to change her position whenever she likes to do so. During the first stage of normal labour, the majority of mothers prefer to be sitting, standing or walking, i.e. with the trunk almost vertical, and to move freely changing from one vertical position to another. Very few choose to be lying in bed all the time, although some would lie horizontally for short periods.

Several mothers have given positive patterns. One such example of such patterns is to sit between uterine contractions and stand up during each contraction, embracing her husband. Others walk between contractions and stand still during the contraction. Some mothers ask for massage in the suprapubic or sacroiliac areas during uterine contractions.'

One answer to the problems of restricted movements is the use of telemetry, but this is not wholly adequate. The mother has to have an electrode inserted in her baby's scalp. To make this possible she will have had her membranes ruptured, and this means that every time she moves amniotic fluid cascades down her leg and thus restricts her movements. She has a band round her leg and she has to carry a heavy piece of equipment like a shoulder bag. Her movements are limited in that she cannot go for a walk because she may go out of range of the monitor. So, although the use of telemetry makes continuous electronic fetal monitoring slightly more acceptable, it is still very restricting.

The most acceptable alternative in many units (given that once an expensive piece of equipment has been purchased, there is a lot of pressure to use it to justify having spent the money) is to monitor the fetal heart for 20 minutes to half an hour when the woman comes into the labour ward. This provides a baseline against which further readings can be measured or judged.

The woman can then be monitored with a Pinard's stethoscope or Sonicaid/doptone intermittently throughout her labour. This is less restrictive and means that the midwife can be alerted to any deviations from normal and can then react accordingly.

For the 20–30 minutes that the woman is being monitored, she can be encouraged to move to the most comfortable position. If she has to be monitored constantly, she can also be encouraged to take up whatever position is most comfortable within the radius of the flex from the monitor.

It is as well to remember the effect that lying back in a bed has on the oxygenation of the baby in the uterus. The heavy uterus is pressed back and constricts the blood flow in the inferior vena cava and the ascending aorta, the two great blood vessels running up inside the abdominal cavity. This impedes the blood flow to the uterus and ultimately to the baby.

If the woman is able to take up a vertical position, the uterus is tipped forward during contractions and the blood supply to the baby is unimpeded. When the woman is upright, the baby's head is pressed by gravity on to the cervix, so aiding cervical dilatation. When the mother moves her pelvis, she is both increasing her pelvic diameters and helping to rotate the baby into the most favourable position.

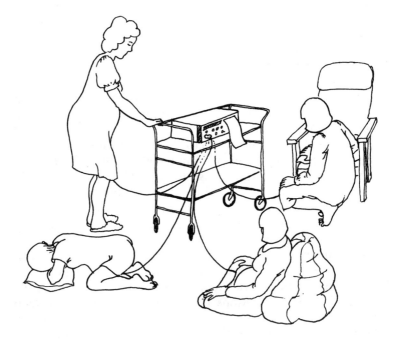

Often husbands or labour partners can be asked to mark the contractions on the monitor. This saves the woman from having yet another belt round her abdomen to measure uterine contractions.

Small portable Sonicaids/doptones are incredibly useful for monitoring the fetal heart when a woman wants to be on her hands and knees as when she is in that position it is almost impossible to listen with a Pinard. The large fetal monitor can also be used for the same function if the ultrasound cardiotocograph is used.

When the woman lies in the bath, a Pinard's stethoscope can be used if the woman raises her tummy up to the midwife. Again, the only disadvantage is that the midwife tends to get her hair wet!

Fetal monitoring may or may not be right for the woman you are looking after in labour. Each case has to be looked at according to its own parameters. With sensitivity and awareness, the midwife can make the monitoring less restrictive, less frequent, less invasive.

References and Further Reading

Balaskas, A., Balaskas, J. (1982). *Active Birth Manifesto*. London: Active Birth Movement.

Caldeyro-Barcia, R. (1979). *Physiological and Psychological Bases for the Modern and Humanised Management of Normal Labour.* Scientific Publication No. 858 of the Centro Latinoamericano de Perinatologia y Desarrollo Humano. Available from Centro Latinoamerican de Perinatologia y Desarrollo Human, Casilla de Correo 627, Montevideo, Uruguay, and from the NCT.

Central Midwives Board, Central Midwives Board for Scotland, Northern Ireland Council for Nurses & Midwives, and An Bord Altranais. (1983) *The Role of the Midwife.*

Dunn, P. M. (1976). Obstetric delivery today. For better or worse? *The Lancet*; 1(1963): 790–3. (April 10).

Haverkamp, A. D., Orleans, M., Langendoerfer, S., McFee, J. G., Murphy, J. (1976). A controlled trial of the differential effects of intrapartum fetal monitoring. *American Journal of Obstetrics and Gynaecology*; 125(3): 310–20.

Haverkamp, A. D., Thompson, II. E., McFee, J. G., Cetrulo, C. (1976). The evaluation of continuous fetal heart rate monitoring in high-risk pregnancy. *American Journal of Obstetrics and Gynaecology*; 125(3): 310.

Inch, S. (1982). *Birthrights*. London: Hutchinson Ltd.

Kelso, I. M., Parsons, R. J., Lawrence, G. F., Arora, S. S., Edmonds,

D. K., Cooke, I. D. (1978). An assessment of continuous fetal heart rate monitoring in labor. A randomized trial. *American Journal of Obstetrics and Gynaecology*; 131: 526.

MacDonald, D., Grant, A., Sheridan-Pereira, M., Boylan, P., Chalmers, I. (1985). The Dublin randomized controlled trial of intrapartum fetal heart rate monitoring. *American Journal of Obstetrics and Gynaecology*; 152(5): 524–39 (July).

Renou, P., Chang, A., Anderson, I., Wood, C. (1976). Controlled trial of fetal intensive care. *American Journal of Obstetrics and Gynaecology*; 126: 470.

Wood, C. (1978). A comparison of two controlled trials concerning the efficacy of fetal intensive care. *Journal of Perinatal Medicine*; 6: 149.

Chapter Eight

Suturing

After a delivery the woman's perineum often needs a few stitches, and it is a great satisfaction to the midwife if she can do the suturing herself. It means that she can complete the delivery. It also means that she can make sure that the woman has adequate analgesia for the suturing and that the suturing is done gently, with sensitivity and soon after delivery. Furthermore, if the midwife goes on seeing the woman she has delivered, providing care in the puerperium, she will be aware of what happens to a woman when she has sutured her and she can keep an eye on her suturing technique.

Obviously it is best if suturing can be avoided. A woman should be encouraged antenatally to try to stretch her perineum as much as possible by practising squatting, sitting tailor fashion and massaging her perineum with olive oil.

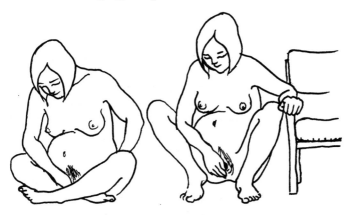

During labour, splitting can be avoided and the tissues made softer and more stretchy by being massaged with clean oiled hands. Often partners or the woman herself can do this. The midwife may find it difficult to fit it in with listening to the fetal heart and putting on sterile gloves, but it could be something that the assisting midwife could do. Furthermore, it is really valuable for her to find out what the perineum feels like.

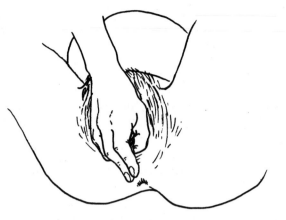

Another thing which appears to help stretching and to prevent tearing is a hot pad applied to the perineum when it is very stretched by the baby's head. The easiest thing to use is a sanitary towel soaked in very hot water. Women seem to find this very comforting even though I use it quite hot.

Sometimes a tear is unavoidable, but an episiotomy is nearly always avoidable. Remember that (unless the baby is in danger) the rule for episiotomies is wait and then wait again and then wait some more.

Whether you are suturing a tear or an episiotomy, at first you will be nervous. You will wonder whether this woman will ever be the same again, whether she will ever feel sexual pleasure again, whether your work will cripple her for years. While you are distressing yourself with all these thoughts, remember that, if it were not you suturing her, it could easily be a medical student and she or he might well be handling a needle for the first time. I often think of my 20 year old son when I see medical students suturing women. He is not vastly different from most young men of his generation — charming, macho, a real smoothie (he *is* very delicious though). To my knowledge he has never sewn a button on. His mother is too bolshie to sew them on for him, so he bribes his girlfriends or his sister — 'Bo, if you sew this for me, I'll give you fifty pence'. If he were a medical student, he could be sewing a woman's perineum — learning how to sew on the most sensitive part of a woman's anatomy! You may not be a whizz at complicated embroidery, but I bet you have sewn a few buttons on.

The great advantage of where you are sewing is that it is very vascular. It heals quickly and completely given patience, time, a good diet and pelvic floor muscle exercises. I often think that women can have better pelvic floors following childbirth because they learn about pelvic floor exercise.

The importance of exercise has been shown by Gordon and Logue from Northwick Park Hospital. They looked at five groups of women — women who had had episiotomies, women who had intact perinea after delivery, women who had had second degree tears, women who had had caesarean sections and women who were nulliparous. The most significant effect on strong pelvic floor muscles was exercise. Pelvic floor exercises were good but even better was more general exercise —keep fit, jogging, running, swimming and dancing.

Hopefully you are now feeling slightly less nervous than before about suturing this perineum. Before doing anything else, however, it is important to look at the woman's genitalia to see what suturing, if any, she needs. Some midwives are taught to examine the cervix following delivery. When a woman is as exquisitely sensitive as she is following delivery, I think it is an act of great barbarity to grope up her vagina to look at her cervix. If there is a cervical tear, there will have been abnormal occurrences earlier — a very long second stage, a difficult forceps delivery, a woman pushing on a cervix which is not fully dilated. In a normal labour, it is *highly unlikely* that the woman's cervix will be torn. A woman's body is beautifully constructed and usually works well. Only if the woman is bleeding excessively with a well-contracted uterus should the cervix be examined.

Looking at the genitalia after delivery is always rather shocking for the observer. The whole area is swollen and seems enormous. The rugae (folds) of the vagina seem to be hanging out and there may be swollen haemorrhoids. First, ask the woman to tighten her pelvic floor muscles. Often she will be able to do this and you will feel cheered that her muscles are alive and well under this swollen area. If the woman has lacerations on her labia, the kindest thing is to leave them unless they are actually pouring blood. Sutures in such a sensitive area are very uncomfortable, and this area heals within about 48 hours.

If they are bleeding profusely, it is often better to clamp the bleeding vessels with very fine mosquito forceps. This will stop the flow and after about five minutes you can take the clamps off and the bleeding will have ceased altogether.

Having examined the woman and seen whether she actually does need sutures or not, you need to get her into a position in which it is easy for you to see and where you can have a good light on the whole area. Many women are put up into stirrups for suturing. This is very uncomfortable, makes women feel very vulnerable, and it is totally unnecessary. With the usual type of delivery bed, it is very easy to get women into a position which is good for suturing without resorting to stirrups.

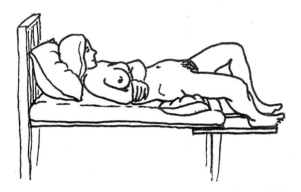

The woman should be asked to lie on the bed. A pillow should be placed under her bottom, and her bottom should be at the edge of the pillow so that it is almost overhanging the edge of the pillow. Both bottom and pillow should be brought to where the bed divides. The bed should be divided so that the woman can rest her feet on the tray which is made when the end of the bed is not quite fully pushed in.

Find yourself a stool and aim a light towards the perineum. Make sure that the woman is comfortable. With washed hands you open the suture pack and pour your antiseptic lotion into the relevant receptacle. You should then open a 10 ml ampoule of lignocaine 1% and open the syringe and needle, dropping them onto the sterile field untouched. The sutures should also be opened and dropped onto the sterile field.

Wash your hands, put on a pair of sterile gloves and draw up the lignocaine into the syringe. Check again that the woman is comfortable, that she has enough pillows under her

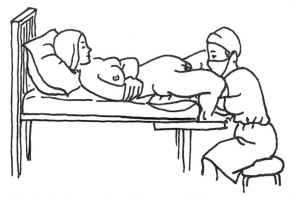

head, that the baby is comfortably in its father's arms, and then scrub up.

Having put on a sterile gown and sterile gloves (these need to fit closely), wash the woman down with antiseptic, talking to her all the time.

'Jane, what I am going to do is wash you down with this warmed lotion. Is that cool enough? Now I'm going to put a sterile sheet underneath you. Can you lift your bottom up?'

The soothing sound of your voice will act as a distraction and a calming influence. You should try to talk throughout the procedure, because she will feel very nervous and she will be reassured by your voice. If you are feeling nervous too, you will also be reassured by your voice.

Next you need to anaesthetise the woman. She will be very nervous about the needle going into her, and it is best done smoothly and speedily. The only disadvantage of the woman being in this position is that it is almost impossible to infiltrate from below the tear — you will need to infiltrate from the top of the tear on both sides. Direct the needle to the base of the tear until the needle is in up to the shaft. Draw back to make sure you are not in a blood vessel and then slowly push the plunger in as you bring the needle up. You will see the slight swelling of the tissues as you put the lignocaine in.

You need to do the same on the other side of the tear. Try to leave a small amount of lignocaine in the syringe in case the woman needs some more later.

Now you need to wait a short while for the lignocaine to take effect. Reassure the woman that you will not start doing

anything else until the local anaesthetic has taken effect.
Meanwhile get all your equipment ready. After a few minutes,
try touching the tear and, if the woman is anaesthetised, you
can start.

The first very useful thing to do is to insert a tampon into the
vagina to keep the area dry and as free of blood as possible. It is
useful to clip a small Spencer Wells artery forceps on the end of
the tape so that you remember that the tampon is there.

The basic principle for suturing the perineum is:

- Sew up the insides of the vagina first.
- Then sew the muscle together.
- Finish by sewing up the outer skin.

The basic principle with holding the needle in a needle holder is
always to have the needle at right angles to the needle holder.

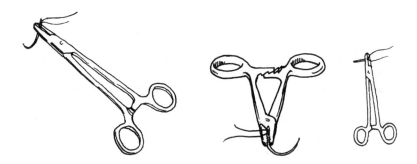

You put the first stitch at the very end (apex) of the tear, sew
the two sides of skin together and then tie a knot. Many people
are absolutely flummoxed by knots and there are several worthy
tomes which have highly complicated drawings of knots with
little arrows pointing in several directions all at the same time.
Many doctors and midwives pride themselves on their one-
handed knots — quick and simple knots done with a pair of
forceps — and on several other impressive-looking and
dashingly-executed knots. Calm yourself with the thought of
what this knot is supposed to do. It is supposed to keep the
catgut together, and this can just as easily be done with a reef
knot tied three times. The principle to remember is:

- Right over left.
- Left over right.
- Right over left again.
        or
- Left over right.
- Right over left.
- Left over right again.

Triple knot

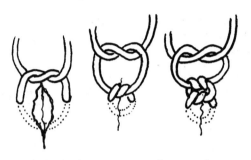

To suture the skin of the vagina, the simplest way is to insert the needle just under the skin on one side of the tear, and take it across just under the skin of the other side of the tear. Reinsert the needle about 4 or 5 mm along, insert the needle just under the skin and takes it across under the skin of the other side of the tear. You now have two ends on the same side. Tie your reef knot three times and cut the ends.

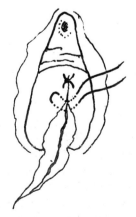

Carry on up inside the vagina until you come to the little ridge which signals the end of the vaginal mucosa and the beginning of the outside skin (fourchette). You are now left with a hole into the muscle. Take your curved needle (taking care to hold it at right angles in the needle holder) and take it through a full circle and then tie each knot individually to hold the muscle together. You will need about three of these sutures into the muscle. Then feel into it with your finger and, if there is still some hole left, put in another suture until you are left with no hole.

 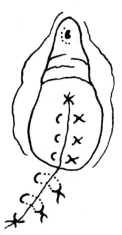

Now suture the remaining skin on the outside of the perineum. This can be sutured in the same way that you sutured the inside of the vagina.

One of the common mistakes of the inexperienced suturer is to put in too many sutures. When the swelling of the tissues subsides, the sutures take up too much flesh and impede healing. Obviously you need to put in enough sutures, but too many is worse, not better.

After suturing, insert a finger into the woman's anus to check that no sutures have strayed into there. If they have it is imperative that the sutures are removed and that you start again, because they can make a sinus through from the vagina to the anus. While you are inserting your finger into the woman's anus, it is also a good idea to try to reduce any haemorrhoids she might have. Point out to her what you are doing and that, if she keeps pushing them up into her anus, they will eventually go completely once the effects of progesterone have tapered off.

Remove the tampon (this can be half a sanitary towel if you have no tampons), and then encourage the woman to tighten her pelvic floor muscles. Let her know when you can see an effect so that she knows when she is doing it correctly. Wash her down and you have finished.

Women are very sensitive about their perinea — with good reason. Following most normal deliveries and, with no undue trauma, many women will feel a dragging aching feeling in their pelvic floor if they stand for any length of time. This can be relieved with more rest and just with the passage of time. Many women also feel a throbbing and aching of their clitoris for a couple of weeks following delivery. Most women experience backache for some months following delivery. This can also be helped by adopting the right posture and more rest.

Haemorrhoids invariably disappear within a couple of weeks. If they are very swollen, they can be helped by the application of an ice pack, by the woman lying on her front whenever possible, by plenty of baths, by KY jelly, by lignocaine gel, by trying to reduce them whenever possible, and by patience.

Varicose veins of the vulva, which can be large and aching and throbbing before delivery, completely disappear during labour when the perineum is very stretched by the baby's head. So they cause no problems during delivery, and after delivery they will have disappeared.

Women should be encouraged to keep their stitches as clean and dry as possible. They should be encouraged to wash their perineum. This needs to be demonstrated because most women are extremely frightened of touching the area and, although they give themselves a good soak in the bath, they are too frightened to get a soaped hand and massage their perineum. Massaging, in fact, should be encouraged. Once a woman has got over her fear of touching this injured part of her, she can begin to reclaim it as hers. Furthermore, the massage encourages the circulation in the whole area and probably helps healing. Drying the area is probably best done with tissues or kitchen roll because the woman will be bleeding heavily for the first few days.

The words we use for describing the perineum are very important. I have seen the effect on a woman when a midwife has gazed at her perineum and pronounced 'It's gaping'. It is enough to shatter the woman's confidence in herself as a sexual being for years. Also, think of the effect of such phrases as 'It's broken down', 'It's infected', 'God, what a botch up', 'You look a mess', 'Heavens, who sutured you? They didn't know what they were doing'. What you say must always be chosen to increase the woman's confidence in this part of her body — 'Can you tighten up your pelvic floor for me please?'

- Golly, that's good. I can really see your muscles working.
- It's healing slowly. You are keeping it lovely and clean. Are you giving it a good massage with a soapy hand? Like this.
- Well it's looking very good. It'll soon be completely healed and your muscles will be even stronger than before with you exercising them.
- Oh yes, lovely. You don't look as if you've had a baby at all down there. It's healed so beautifully.'

It is important for women to get enough rest and often they do not realise how much they are doing. Many women continue to watch television until about midnight before going to bed. They are then woken up twice during the night to feed the baby. They omit to have a rest in the afternoon because they have visitors or want to go out, and they end up almost paralytic with exhaustion. A midwife needs at times to be fairly bossy and organising to ensure that women get some rest during the 24 hours.

As well as tightening her pelvic floor muscles in the normal way (as if stopping a stream of urine), there are some exercises which can help strengthen the whole of the pelvic area.

Many women have stress incontinence of urine for a few months after childbirth. Exercise can help enormously here as can encouragement that it will not last for ever.

Here are some exercises to strengthen pelvic floor muscles.

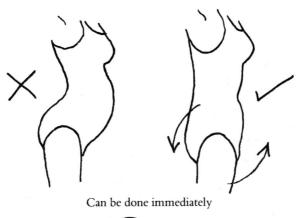

Can be done immediately

To be done from six weeks after the birth

Rotate ten times in each direction

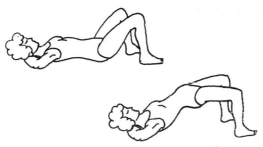

Raise pelvis ten times as slowly as possible

Raise pelvis ten times as slowly as possible

Lift pelvis ten times as slowly as possible

Some women want to make love very soon after childbirth. Having a baby seems to release a huge wave of sexuality, and they could almost eat their man whole. But, even when women have had no perineal trauma, the vagina can often be quite sore during lovemaking, and it can help to have some jelly handy to increase lubrication and to try different positions so that penetration is at a different angle.

For many women the exact opposite occurs. Their body feels totally numb and devoid of any sexual feelings. This can continue for at least a year following delivery. These women need reassuring that they will regain their sexual feelings eventually. They should be encouraged to embrace their partner and to ask him to embrace her. They will need a lot of caressing and courting to light their sexual fires again. If they do manage to have sexual intercourse, they will need a lubricating gel for some time after the birth.

Childbirth is an enormous emotional experience. It is also a physical marathon. Many women do not feel totally 'themselves' for at least a year following delivery. They need encouragement and support. Their life has changed completely. Nothing will ever be the same again. The earth has moved and they need time to find their new place on this altered earth — their place is there but some women take longer than others to find it.

References and Further Reading

Gordon, H., Logue, M. (1985). Perineal muscle function after childbirth. *The Lancet*; 2: 123–5. (July).

Kitzinger, S. (1983). *Woman's Experience of Sex*. London: Dorling Kindersley Ltd. (Also published in paperback in 1985 by Penguin Books.)

Sleep, S. (1984). Epistiotomy in normal delivery — management of the perineum. *Nursing Times*; 80(47): 28–30 (November 21), and *Nursing Times*; 80(48): 51–4 (November 28).

Sleep, J., Grant, A., Garcia, J., Elbourne, D., Spencer, J., Chalmers, I. (1984). West Berkshire perineal management trial. *British Medical Journal*; 289: 587–90 (September 8).

Chapter Nine

Instrumental Deliveries

To have a caesarean section or a forceps delivery is for many women the cause of much grief and anguish. Rationally they know that they have a lovely healthy baby and that, for safety, this baby probably needed to be delivered by medical means. Nonetheless the way the child was delivered often causes extreme distress.

The way our bodies work is terribly important to us. You only have to think of the distress a man suffers when he cannot achieve an erection or the anguish women go through when they are unable to conceive. Even in the days when it was easier to adopt a baby, women were still distraught when they could not become pregnant. They wanted a baby and they wanted it to come from their own body — they wanted their body to work.

It would seem that the anguish women suffer when they have to be induced, accelerated, delivered by forceps or delivered by caesarean section is part of this feeling that their body is not *working* properly — that somehow they have failed as a woman.

Often antenatal groups such as the National Childbirth Trust or the Active Birth Movement are criticised for making women feel that they have failed when their bodies have not worked as they wished. These groups are accused of giving women too high expectations of childbirth. But any midwife knows that women who have never been to a National Childbirth Trust class in their lives still feel the same. The difference is that women who have been to antenatal groups learn to identify and articulate their feelings much more easily than they could before. The wonderful value of these groups is that they help their members to respect themselves and their own wishes and feelings.

Women have a great yearning and need for their bodies to work and, when their childbirth is taken over from them, they need to grieve that loss. Their rational mind tells them that it was the only way their baby could have been delivered.

Everyone around them tells them that 200 years ago they would have been dead if they had been in the same situation without access to a safe caesarean section. But it really makes very little difference to their feelings. They may be extremely grateful to the surgeon and the midwives and they may be thrilled with their baby, but still they will feel very distressed and no amount of reassurance and reasoning will help them. They need other women who have experienced the same pain to talk to and to show them that they are not alone or going mad, that other women feel the same.

Today caesareans are done much more frequently than ever before. Nationally one out of every nine women has a caesarean. In some hospitals this can reach one in six, and in some hospitals in the US the proportion has reached one in three.

Women in this day and age have even more problems with caesareans than women years ago. They know that caesareans are done much more frequently than before. They know that caesareans, which were always done as a very last resort in the past, are now seen by many doctors as an acceptable alternative to vaginal birth. So when a woman is told during her labour that she has to have a caesarean section, she often doubts whether she really needs it, but she feels that she is not in a position to resist. Alternatively, her doubts may not come until some while later.

It is likely that caesarean sections will increase the more we medicalise labour, the more we alienate a woman from her body, the more we frighten her with our own fear. The more we interrupt her labour, the more likely she is not to progress in labour, to labour wearily on for hours, for her baby to pick up her distress and show this with his heartbeat. To labour normally, women need to feel loved and cherished. They need complete privacy. They need to be able to abandon and surrender themselves to their labour. They need to know the midwife with them so that they are filled with trust, and they can more easily surrender themselves, if outside stimuli (light, sounds, smells) are removed.

Modern labour wards are usually the antithesis of the sort of atmosphere a woman needs in which to labour well. What is especially poignant about this is that the people working inside most modern labour wards, the midwives and doctors, are committed, caring, compassionate people doing the very best that they can for women, but working against incredible odds. They look after women who are total strangers to them and to whom they are total strangers. They work in labour rooms which as Kitzinger has described, sometimes resemble Piccadilly Circus with people 'popping in' to borrow equipment, to see what is going on, to offer to 'take over for a while' so that the attending midwife can have a coffee break. They work in rooms which have a grille in the window just like prison windows, so that every now and then the woman looks up and sees a pair of eyes looking in on her.

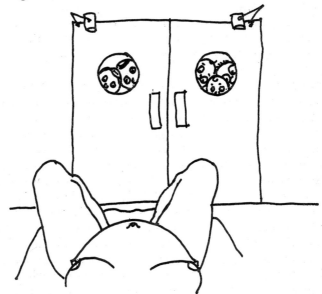

All this is so counterproductive to the passage of normal labour that it is a tribute to the indomitability of the human spirit that so many babies are born normally and indeed that for many women the birth of their baby even in these circumstances is an enjoyable and wonderful experience.

Until we change the environment in which we expect women to give birth and until *all* those involved with women and their childbirth respect each woman and her beautifully designed body, we shall continue with the conflict that so many women feel about childbirth at the moment. Women feel that they have been taken over and that they are losing control of themselves and their bodies. This, as we know from the work of Oakley, has psychological consequences. Women who are midwives feel desperate at what is happening to the women they are with — the women who could be their sisters, their friends, themselves.

So what can the sensitive midwife do to help a woman if she has to have a caesarean section or instrumental delivery? If she is actually *with* the woman, has been there through the labour and will be there for the rest of the labour, the most important thing for her to do is to explain fully what is going to happen, not just once but several times because the woman will be tired and shocked and probably will not hear what is said to her the first few times.

'Jane, the baby is very tired and so are you, so the doctor is going to help the baby out with forceps. First of all we shall put your legs up in these stirrups. Just imagine that you've got your legs resting on a dining room chair. Then we shall put a very fine tube up into your bladder. This shouldn't hurt but it will feel very peculiar. It will tap off any urine in your bladder. Then the doctor will give you an injection of local anaesthetic into your vagina to numb it — just like the dentist does to your mouth when you have your teeth done — and when it's numb he will insert two sides of the forceps around the baby's head. The forceps will cradle the baby's head and then he will gently and firmly guide the baby's head out while you try and push. It will feel horrid for you as if your whole insides are coming out but I will hold you in my arms, and together we will count up to 85, and by the time we've counted it will all be over and the baby will be here.'

Having both her lover's and her midwife's arms around her will help the woman. Her partner will need to be helped to do this because he will feel out of place and in the way, but his familiar arms and his lovely familiar smell to nestle into will help the woman through the horrid but short forceps delivery. Women are often more comfortable if the operator can stop every now and then for her to catch her breath. The counting of a predefined number is helpful because it makes the ordeal finite and the woman knows that it will all be over in what amounts to just over a minute. The midwife needs to control the rate of the counting, otherwise the woman will count to 85 so quickly that she will have finished before the operator. It is often useful to suggest counting to a 100 and say that it is likely that you will not get to more than about 85.

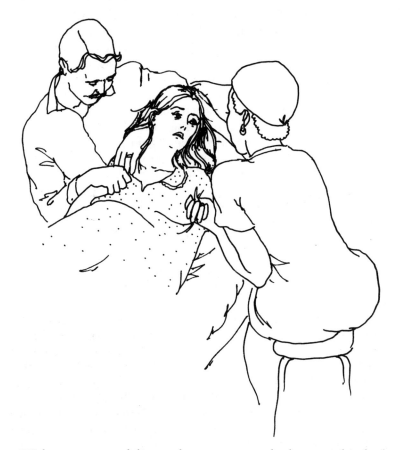

With a ventouse delivery the woman needs the same kind of explanation. The insertion of the cup is not as traumatic as the insertion of forceps (which for many women feels like a violation or rape but at least is mercifully short). The insertion of the ventouse cup takes longer and is a much more leisurely business. The woman also seems to feel much more a part of the whole procedure as if she is being helped to *give* birth rather than having a baby extracted from her.

When a woman has an epidural in situ she needs just as much reassurance as any other woman. She is also helped enormously by being cradled in loving arms while she is going through the experience and by having soothing crooning words said to her. 'That's right, Jane. That's right. Be lovely and relaxed. That's

good. The baby's coming. It's nearly over now. It's nearly the
baby's birthday. Not long now, nearly over. You're so brave.
You're so good. What a lucky baby to have such an amazing
mother who is prepared to go through all this for him. Such a
lucky baby, such a lucky baby — now the baby's head is out,
the worst bit's over, clever you, brilliant woman.'

The involvement of the midwife with a woman who is having
a caesarean section is more complex, mainly because more
midwives are involved in the proceedings.

If you are the midwife who has been with the woman during
labour or prior to her elective section, your main duty is to
explain over and over again exactly what is going to happen.

'Now Nasreen, what I am going to do now is I'm going to shave
your pubic hair away, so that there isn't any hair where the
doctors are going to do the caesarean. Then I'm going to put a
very fine tube up into your bladder, which will feel very peculiar
but I'll help you to relax so that it doesn't feel too strange. Then
we'll put an operation nightdress on you and then I'm going to
give you something very bitter to drink to make the acid in your
stomach less strong.

The next thing we shall do is go to the operating theatre

together. You will be lying on a bed on wheels. Ravi, you can't come inside the operating theatre but if you take that chair over there you can sit outside, and the minute the baby is born (which will be about 25 minutes after we go inside the theatre), I'll bring it out for a cuddle with its Dad.

Now Nasreen, when we go into the theatre, it is all very shiny and metallic. The doctors will put a drip into your arm first of all, and then they will ask you to breathe through a mask. It won't make you go to sleep because it is oxygen for the baby. All the time this is happening to you, the midwives and doctors will be getting ready for the operation. They will be scrubbing their hands and putting on green gowns and sterile gloves. The midwife who hands the instruments to the doctors will be getting all the instruments ready and they will clink and clank a bit. Then we shall bandage a piece of tinfoil to your leg, and then they will wash down your tummy with some antiseptic. All this will be done when you are still awake. I will be there and I will hold your hand all the time.

When it is time for you to go to sleep, the doctor will put the anaesthetic in through your vein and I will tell you when he is going to do that. You will just go off to sleep and the next thing you will know is that I shall be saying to you "Wake up, Nasreen. Here's your baby". And it will all be over and your baby will be born.'

Once in the theatre it is important to give Nasreen a running commentary on what is happening. She will find the sound of your voice very comforting, and the holding of her hand is of paramount importance — having an operation is the nearest brush with death that most of us experience in our lives. We are literally giving our body up to the care of another. Most people feel that they will never wake up after an operation, that the end has come. To have the physical comforting of another at this time can make all the difference in the world.

Ravi will be worried to death outside the room and it is kind to keep him informed of progress and to introduce the baby to him as soon as feasible.

The midwife who is scrubbing has yet another role to play. Many midwives find it extremely difficult to learn to scrub for a caesarean section. Many of us are frightened of operations and theatres. We chose our profession because we like normality and health, not sickness and people being cut open. But sometimes a caesarean has to be done, and it is useful if we can try to make the experience as positive for the parents as possible.

If at all possible it is good if the scrub midwife can meet the parents prior to the operation. She can also explain the whole procedure to them both. The more the mother is taken through the whole experience, the less shocked she will be by it and the easier she will find it to assimilate.

The scrub midwife should explain that she will be wearing a green gown, mask and hat and that only her eyes will show. Her name is Doreen and she will keep an eye on what the baby does when he or she is born, and she will come back and tell Nasreen all about it tomorrow. If Ravi has a camera with him, she might also suggest that she will arrange someone in the theatre to take photos of the baby as it emerges and during its first few minutes. It is also very useful to take photos of the baby when he first meets his mother. Nasreen will think she has dreamt that first meeting with her baby, but if she has photos of the baby lying beside her, it will help to reinforce her memories. In her perceptive study of women having a caesarean section under general anaesthetic, Judith Trowell shows that they had a period of amnesia for 19 hours following the operation.

Trowell's work looked at a group of socially advantaged women, who lived in their own homes, who had a stable relationship with the father of their babies, and who had emergency caesarean sections for ambiguous reasons such as failure to progress. She found that compared to a matched control group, the women who had experienced a caesarean were more depressed, more anxious, lacking in confidence in their mothering abilities, took longer to perceive their children as identifiable personalities, found their children more difficult at three years old, had less eye-to-eye contact and showed less appropriate and sensitive mothering behaviour. The children, however, appeared to be no different from each other, whether they had been born normally or by caesarean section.

In her abstract Trowell suggests that 'There must be serious doubts about the need for an emergency caesarean delivery in this sample. They were a problem group of women as difficult to follow up as to deliver. In their histories there was a trend towards more difficulties in their past and present relationships. Did they need more sensitive handling during delivery to avoid an emergency caesarean section? Professionals frequently find anxiety hard to bear and need to act rather than attempt to understand the origin of the pain. It is easy to overlook the subtle long-term effects of the action when it appears to solve the immediate problem'.

Is the increase in caesarean sections merely a response to our own anxiety? Or, more likely, the obstetrician's reponse to anxiety? Whatever it is, the woman at the other end of the procedure needs all our support and cherishing to go through this ordeal.

The scrub midwife has been to meet the woman. She has arranged about photographing the baby as he or she arrives into the world. She rings and contacts an anaesthetist. She arranges for cross-matched blood to be fetched, for a paediatrician to be present at delivery, for an assistant to run to fetch missing items and to count with her, and for an operating department assistant if available to help the anaesthetist. She puts on a mask, protective cap and overshoes and goes into the theatre and checks the resuscitaire for the baby — that all equipment is there and ready. She undoes the outer wrap of the caesarean pack which is laid out on a trolley next to the operating table. Next to the trolley, she has a Mayo table and two bowl carriers. Then the midwife puts a gown pack out and a pair of sterile gloves and she begins to scrub up.

Scrubbing up consists of washing the hands and forearms for five minutes, starting with soap and water and going on to an iodine or chlorhexidine wash. The hands and forearms are held with the hands upwards so that the water and antiseptic runs off the elbows rather than the fingers. Five minutes is always longer than you think, so the clock needs to be watched to make sure the hands and arms have been thoroughly washed. A sterilised scrubbing brush is used to scrub the nails and between the fingers. The soap and antiseptic is rinsed off with the hands held up throughout.

In the gown pack will be two paper towels, one for drying the left hand and one for the right, drying from the hands up to the elbows. The scrub midwife then puts on her sterilised gown and the runner does up the back for her. The midwife puts on her sterile gloves and moves over to the trolley where she opens the caesarean pack further until it is fully open. She puts a sterile waterproof sheet on the Mayo table and then covers that with a

Mayo cover. She now has two sterile work surfaces — the trolley and the Mayo table.

With the runner nurse the midwife checks and counts the instruments which are inside the sterile pack. The runner nurse writes them up on a board for checking later. She also writes up the number of swabs and they are counted together.

In the pack it is likely that they will have —

CAESAREAN SECTION PACK

8 Long sponge holders
10 Towel clips
2 Bard Parker handles
1 Non-toothed Waughs forceps
2 Non-toothed forceps
2 Toothed Bonneys forceps
1 Nurse's scissors
1 Straight Mayo scissors
1 McIndoes scissors
1 Curved Mayo scissors
1 Umbilical scissors
5 Small straight artery forceps
10 Large straight Spencer Wells artery forceps
6 Green Armitage Forceps
2 Kocker forceps
2 Allis tissue forceps
2 Lanes tissue forceps
2 Mayo needle holders
1 Diathermy forceps ⎫ both in a quiver
1 Diathermy lead ⎭
1 Poole sucker ⎫ with sucker tubing
1 Yankeur sucker ⎭
2 Medium Langenbeck retractors
1 Morris retractor
1 Doyens retractor
1 Wrigleys forceps
1 Michel clip gallery and applicator
2 Strips double 12 mm Michel clips
1 Redivac introducer
Swabs and towels
2 Bundles of 5 medium gauze swabs

2 Bundles of 5 abdominal swabs
1 Sanitary towel
3 Paper macs
4 Small towels
3 Large towels
1 Mayo cover
1 Perfex cloth

When all the instruments have been counted (they will all be clipped together in large clips) and written up on the board, and when the abdominal packs and swabs have been counted and written up on the board, the scrub midwife can then begin to prepare her trolley.

She must throw nothing away. The cord around each group of swabs must be carefully counted and put in a safe place on her trolley. The outsides of the suture materials must be kept together.

In the bowl packs will be some receivers and gallipots. Each receiver is used for a different purpose.

- One receiver has a gallipot containing antiseptic solution in it and about five sponge holders with swabs on them — for washing down the woman's abdomen.

- One receiver contains two gallipots — one for holding the suture materials and one for holding them when they are finished with.

- One receiver holds the Bark Parker handles — now with blades on them.

- One receiver is given to the runner for collecting soiled instruments and swabs.

The runner nurse opens up the required sutures and drops them onto the trolley. Each surgeon will have his or her preference, and most units will have each surgeon's requirements and glove size written down. They will also have written down whether the surgeon is right or left handed, which alerts the scrub midwife as to which hand to pass the instruments to.

The sutures needed are as the body requires when suturing up —

- Thick sutures for the uterus.
- Fine sutures for the peritoneum.

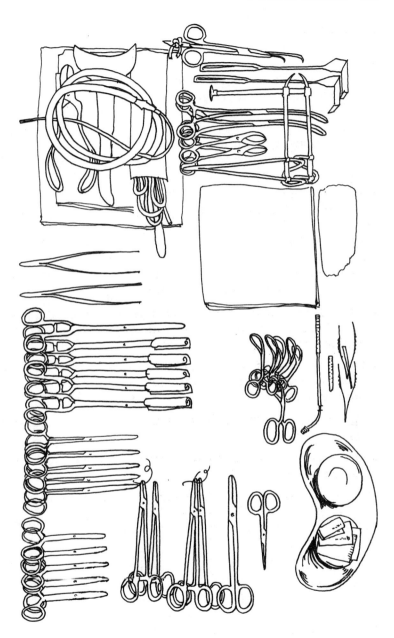

- Sutures for the fat layer.
- Sutures for the rectus sheath.
- Skin sutures (or clips or a prolene thread).

While the woman is being brought to theatre and the surgeons and anaesthetist are arriving, the scrub midwife quietly and methodically gets all the instruments which will be needed ready for use.

On the Mayo table, which the surgeons will work from, she lines up the large artery forceps, the scissors, the receiver with the scalpels in it, the towel holders and the tissue forceps.

By this time Nasreen has probably arrived. Doreen greets her and explains that she is just getting everything ready before Nasreen goes to sleep. She reminds Nasreen that she will have her tummy washed with antiseptic before she goes to sleep and she introduces her to the runner nurse who is going to take photos of the baby as he or she is born.

When Nasreen arrived, the runner nurse wrote down on the board the time of the patient's arrival. She will also write down the time the anaesthetic commenced, the time the operation started, the time the baby was born, the time the placenta was delivered and the time the operation finished.

The scrub midwife ensures that the diathermy is set up, that Nasreen has one part bandaged to her leg and that the diathermy lead is connected to the machine. Also she ensures that the sucker is connected up.

The scrub midwife ensures that on the Mayo table are artery forceps, tissue forceps, Wrigleys forceps, Doyens retractor and several abdominal packs as well as the scalpels and scissors — so that the surgeons can just help themselves to the instruments they need.

While Nasreen is having an intravenous line inserted and is holding the oxygen mask to her face, her abdomen is being washed down. While this is being done, it is important to leave Nasreen's gown covering the top of her and a sheet covering her legs. Nothing is more dehumanising than being left naked in an operating theatre, and the woman will lose confidence in her attendants if they do not at all times respect her and her body.

A large towel is put above where the incision will be, and a large towel is put below where the incision will be. A small towel is put either on side of the incision and they are all clipped on with

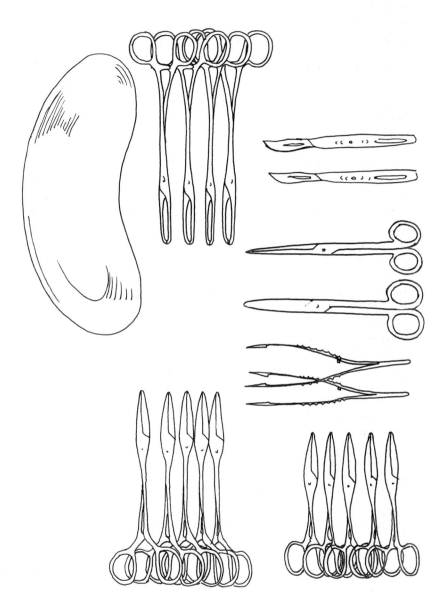

towel clips. By now Nasreen is anaesthetised. As she goes off to sleep, it is helpful to say quietly 'You're going to have your baby now, your baby will soon be born'.

The midwife who was holding her hand now goes and scrubs up ready to take the baby. She needs a mucus extractor and one of the small towels.

The scrub midwife will now push the Mayo table over the end of the operating table and will bring her trolley up to the side of the table so that she has easy access to all the equipment.

The skin is incised with a scalpel, and any bleeding is mopped up with an abdominal pack. Then the rectus sheath and the fat are incised. Scissors are used to incise the peritoneum and then the Doyens retractor is inserted to keep the bladder and skin etc. out of the way. The peritoneum over the uterus is cut with the scissors and then the uterus is incised. As the amniotic fluid comes flowing out, the scrub midwife sucks it up with a sucker. She hands a sterile towel to the midwife who will be taking the baby, and she keeps an eye on what is happening as the baby is delivered so that she can recount it step by step to his mother tomorrow. She reminds the runner nurse to take photos.

Once the baby is born and the cord has been clamped and cut, the midwife taking the baby takes him over to the resuscitaire and the paediatrician. She needs to keep an eye on how the baby is handled and to ensure that he is handled very gently and lovingly and not sucked out too enthusiastically unless it is necessary. The placenta is scooped out and put into a receiver. The sterile bowls have been filled with sterile water by the runner nurse and, when instruments are bloody, they can be washed out in the sterilised water. The baby is taken out to meet his father.

The sucker is used to suck up any spare fluid or blood and so are the abdominal packs. Each time an abdominal pack is discarded, it is hung on a rack, and they are hung in fives to make counting easier.

The suturing up now begins and the scrub midwife hands a non-toothed forcep and suture material (which she has already put on a needle holder) to the surgeon. All the time she and the runner nurse are checking the number of instruments, needles, abdominal packs and swabs that they have. Before the abdomen is closed, a Redivac tube is introduced and a sterile Redivac bottle is dropped onto the trolley by the running nurse. Before the abdomen is closed a very thorough count is made of all instruments, suture needles, packs and swabs so that the scrub midwife can account for every single item.

Once all the suturing has been done, the skin is sprayed with plastic skin and a dressing applied. The Redivac bottle is attached and often the catheter is removed, depending on the surgeon.

Nasreen's anaesthetic is now wearing off, and she is put onto her bed and woken up. Now is the time to fetch Ravi and the baby so Nasreen can see them. Photos should be taken of this moment so that she will have a record of her first meeting with her baby. Nasreen will be terribly sleepy and probably in a lot of pain and will probably need some analgesia. While she is lying on her side, it is useful to put the baby to the breast. One of the most important ways to ensure successful breastfeeding is to get the baby sucking on the breast within the first hour following birth. Nasreen will feel more confident if she has done this at least once, and it will help the baby to get used to sucking. Having said that, not all babies want to suck at this stage so you can only do your best.

Nasreen and her family will be wheeled away. The scrub midwife must now check the placenta, estimate the blood loss, and wash all the instruments ready for repacking for the next caesarean section. She will need to write the case notes in the usual way and the birth register and birth notification. The theatre must be left completely ready for the next caesarean, which may be a dire emergency and may happen in five minutes' time.

Tomorrow the scrub midwife should go to see Nasreen and talk her through the caesarean section, telling her exactly how her baby was born, telling her what the baby did when he was born — whether he cried or passed urine, whether he opened his eyes, whether he whimpered, how he looked and what the people there might have said about him.

Nasreen will be helped by talking through her experience with the midwives and so will Ravi. For him it will have been a very frightening time, full of trepidation and fearful fantasies.

If Nasreen has an epidural caesarean, her experience will obviously be different. She will probably not have any amnesia and will feel very much a part of her baby's birth. But she will need as much reassurance and as much physical contact (hand holding) as with a general anaesthetic. It is also useful for her to have photos of the baby's birth. With an epidural caesarean, it is likely that Ravi will be able to sit next to her and hold her hand so she will feel much more supported.

With epidurals many women find it difficult to breathe or feel very shaky during the operation. They need to be told about this beforehand or reassured while it is happening.

When she is up and about, the woman needs to be given instructions on how to look after her wound and how to clean it. Moir-Bussy, in a paper in the *Journal of Infection Control*, states that 5·1% of women having caesarean sections have minor sepsis, 17·49% have wound inflammation and 1% have major sepsis with wound breakdown.

The woman needs to be helped to come to terms with this scar on her body, to be helped to touch it and to absorb it into herself as part of her new mother's body. Women who have had vaginal deliveries often need the same help coming to terms with their altered genitals — even if the change is so slight that an observer would not be able to see it.

She needs to be congratulated on this act of love on her part — that she was prepared to be operated on for the sake of her baby. She needs to be helped to realise that she has had a major abdominal operation and that the long-term effects of that will be with her for a few months — tiredness, lethargy, aching — all this with a baby to look after too.

References and Further Reading

Moir-Bussy, B., Hutton, R., Thompson, J. (1985). Wound infection after caesarean section. *Journal of Infection Control* in *Nursing Times*; 81(23): 13–4 (June 5).

Oakley, A. (1980). *Women Confined. Towards a Sociology of Childbirth*. Oxford: Martin Robertson.

Trowell, J. (1982). Possible effects of emergency caesarean section on the mother-child relationship. *Early Human Development*; 7: 41–51. Elsevier Biomedical Press.

Trowell, J. (1983). Emergency caesarian section: a research study of the mother/child relationship of a group of women admitted expecting a normal vaginal delivery. *Child Abuse and Neglect*; 7: 387–94.

Chapter Ten

Home Deliveries

To deliver a baby at home is truly to practise as a midwife. To deliver a baby at home is to make decisions, is to tune into your own instincts, is to call up all your knowledge and expertise. To deliver a baby at home is to sometimes feel nervous and alone and a little frightened. It is also to feel strong, to feel humble at the miracle of birth, to stand in awe at the brilliance of cervical dilatation, to wonder at the strength of the human spirit, to admire the ability of women to cope with an incredibly powerful and painful experience, to be delighted at the love between two human beings demonstrated by a loving partner at a birth.

Every year since I have been working as a hospital midwife, I have tried to deliver at least two friends at home. Working inside a hospital affects a midwife. I have found my confidence being chipped away — my confidence in women's bodies, in the marvellous process of labour, in my own instincts as a midwife. This, I now believe, is not the result of actions by any particular people I work with, but is rather the influence of the very institution of the hospital — an institution which represents illness, sickness and pathology, and encourages us to behave in certain ways.

Every time I book a friend for a home delivery I go to see my director of midwifery services and I inform her. I book a holiday when the friend is due so that hopefully the birth takes place when I am off duty. This is important because if I have a contract with an employer, I must keep to that contract, going to work when I am contracted to go. When you think about it, doing home deliveries for a friend could be considered the same as working for an agency, which many midwives do to supplement their income.

I tell my director that I wish to do some home deliveries because, if I am to make the hospital as home-like as possible, I must experience a home delivery from time to time. This, I think, is a very valid reason. In hospital we behave in a certain way. We have strictly defined policies and procedures to carry out. These take away the expertise of the midwife. She is not able to consider or decide on a certain way of dealing with a situation. She has a set of numbered responses which she is ordered to make. Her skills and her instincts are buried under all the in-built 'safeguards' of hospital practice.

I would like to take you step by step through how to deliver a friend at home — in case a friend asks you to deliver her at home. Perhaps it is not until we have delivered someone at home that we realise what being a midwife really is and what childbirth really is too.

YOUR WORK AND CONTRACT

Having booked a holiday for the relevant fortnight, it is also a good idea (if it is feasible) to ask another midwife to be on call with you so that if you should break your leg on the day, she would be able to carry on. I always ask one of the independent midwives to cover me. They offer much professional support to other midwives as well as to the women who are lucky enough to have their services.

YOUR LEGAL OBLIGATIONS

It is essential that you should have your own copy of both the Midwives' Rules and the Midwives' Code of Practice. (They are obtainable from the United Kingdom Central Council for Nursing, Midwifery and Health Visiting, 23 Portland Place, London W1N 3AF.) Go through them both with a marker pen and highlight every rule which affects you and the home delivery you are about to embark upon. Our great strength as a profession is that we have rules and, if we work within those rules, we are protected from incrimination. Midwives at this time have many opponents, not least among their own ranks, and we need at all times to safeguard ourselves. The easiest way to do this is to know and adhere to our rules.

SUPERVISION

The first duty of the midwife is to inform her local supervisor of midwives of her intention to practise, so write to the local supervisor. This is usually the local head of midwifery services but if you have any difficulty finding out, the regional health authority (which is actually the local supervisory authority) will give you her name. Here is an example of the letter you could write.

63 Bayswater Street
Fernbank
Rushbrook C14 12N

Miss Amy Phillips
Supervisor of Midwives
St Reginald's Hospital
Rushbrook C14 4JD

Dear Miss Phillips,   October 19, 1987

I have today booked the following patient for delivery at home with myself acting in an independent capacity.

Ms Holly Francman
23 Holmes Road
Rushbrook, W1

She is expecting her first baby on March 3, 1988.

I have written to her GP, Dr Maxwell of 49 Forbes Road, Rushbrook C4, to ask him if he is willing to provide medical cover for Holly's delivery. I will let you know what his reply is. If he is not willing to be involved, I would anticipate referring Holly to St Reginald's Maternity Unit in the case of any abnormality arising during pregnancy, labour or the puerperium, as this is the nearest obstetric unit.

Could you please send me a Notice of Intention to Practise Form for me to fill in, and could you also send me a Birth Notification Form and a Guthrie Test Form.

Yours sincerely,
Caroline Flint RGN RM No 220364

Send this letter to the supervisor of midwives immediately. Also send a letter to your friend's GP asking him or her if they would be prepared to offer medical cover during the confinement. If you already have a GP who is willing to offer medical cover for your friend, tell the supervisor of midwives. If you know of no GP and your friend's GP is not willing to be involved in a home delivery, *it does not matter. You do not have to have a GP.* You as a midwife can take responsibility for a woman in normal labour. Your duty is to summon a registered medical practitioner should any illness or abnormality of the woman, fetus or baby become apparent. The registered medical practitioner can just as easily be the senior registrar on call at your local maternity unit, whom you ring up to ask for advice, take the woman to for a consultation or summon in the flying squad. In all circumstances the welfare of the mother and baby must be of prime importance for both the midwife and the medical practitioner, so it is essential, if any abnormality should occur, that you refer your friend to a doctor immediately. If the abnormality occurs during pregnancy, is treated and the problem solved, there is no reason for your friend to deliver anywhere else or with anyone else.

BOOKING HISTORY

Many independent midwives use an exercise book for each woman they book. Once they are booking women frequently, they then usually have notes printed or typed. If you are delivering a friend at home, an exercise book should suffice as long as you remember that it is essential to keep the notes forever (well, for 25 years at least) and that if ever you cannot store them, you must give them to the regional health authority in its capacity as the local supervising authority.

On the front of your exercise book write the name of your friend and the date she is due. On the first page write her name, address, telephone number, her date of birth and age, the date of her last menstrual period and the date her baby is due.

Also on the first page write the name of her next of kin or her partner or whoever is relevant and their address and telephone number if different. It is often useful to have work telephone numbers for her and her partner. Write the date of booking and some comment on your friend's home facilities. Also put down the person or people who are going to look after your friend for at least the ten days after delivery — people who will cook meals for her, clean the house or flat, do the washing and fetch the shopping while she lies around, concentrates on the baby, and rests.

It is also useful to put on the first page your friend's blood group and her GP's name, address and telephone number whether or not he or she is going to be involved. You might need to ring the GP in case of any minor illness or infection and you might like a blood sample analysed through the surgery.

It is useful to get to know about this person fully. Ask her to tell you about herself — where she was brought up, whether she has any sisters and brothers, how she first got to know about childbirth. Have a discussion about life with a new baby and the amount of help she is likely to need. Ask about her job and whether there are any hazards to a pregnant woman in her workplace. Ask her about her pleasures, amusements and hobbies. Ask her about how she sees herself as a mother. On the second page and the next few pages, write a complete picture of this woman. If her partner is there, do the same for him. This will take up the first four or five pages of your exercise book.

The next pages can be used for the menstrual history — onset of menstruation, frequency and regularity of menstruation and how long each period lasts — and for the history of previous pregnancies. You need to find out how your friend's mother gave birth because women are often similar to their mothers in the way that they give birth. It is useful to know whether this woman's mother had a good pelvis and how long she took in labour. I often wished I had asked the two primigravid women I delivered at home after only an hour of labour how long their mothers had been, because they both told me afterwards that their mothers had had very short labours. I might not then have been so glib in telling them that it would be hours yet!

Next it is useful to record the couple's medical history, including any serious illnesses (such as rheumatic fever, thromboembolism, renal disease, diabetes, respiratory diseases, tuberculosis, jaundice or sexually transmitted diseases), conditions such as cystitis and thrush, exposure to rubella, any operations, fractures, road accidents involving fractures, psychiatric problems, allergies, and any drugs or medicines being used at the moment.

It is useful to note your friend's height and normal weight and then to turn to the next page and record both families' medical histories — whether both sets of parents are alive and well, whether there is any diabetes, high blood pressure or tuberculosis, whether anyone has had twins, whether there are any inherited disorders in either family and whether there have been any abnormal babies, stillborn babies or babies who died very young.

The next page needs to look at this pregnancy — whether your friend has had any bleeding, infections or urinary problems, how she is feeling now, how she was feeling earlier, whether emotionally she feels any different from usual, how she is eating, whether she needs any iron supplements, whether she has noticed increased vaginal discharge and what it is like, whether she is experiencing excessive salivation, and how she is feeling about this pregnancy.

Get to know whether your friend has any plans for labour and why she wants to have the baby at home.

The next section is the usual:

DATE	WEEKS	PRES & POS	FH	BP	OED	URINE	WT	HB

You will need lots of space on the other side of the page because you will have a lot to put in. When you have an antenatal consultation with a friend, there is so much more to say than at a consultation with a stranger. Leave three double pages' for the antenatal record.

The next two sides of your exercise book should be the beginning and the summary of labour:

Beginning of labour
- Date and time
- History on arrival
- Temperature, pulse, blood pressure
- Urine
- Abdominal palpation
- Vaginal examination

Summary of labour

- Onset of labour
- Midwife called for (date and time)
- Midwife arrived (date and time)

- Dr informed (if GP is involved)
- Dr visited (date and time if he or she does)
- Dr summoned (if applicable)
- Dr visited (date and time if applicable)
- Membranes rupturing (date and time — spontaneous or artificial)
- Liquor
- Os fully dilated (date and time)
- Baby born (date and time)
- Placenta expelled (date and time)
- Length of first stage
- Length of second stage
- Length of third stage
- Blood loss
- Placenta (description)
- Membranes (complete or ragged)
- Cord (number of blood vessels)
- Perineum
- Observations after delivery
- Temperature, pulse, blood pressure
- Uterus (contracted)
- Urine (passed — it is best to stay with your friend until she has passed urine following birth).

On the next pages write a running commentary on the labour. It can be useful to have the same sort of record that you had for the antenatal consultations but with different headings.

DATE/TIME	PULSE	FHR	CONTRACTIONS	BP	URINE

On the opposite page, you can write comments as you go along. For example:

- Mary is standing up in a semi-squat for contractions, being supported by Clifford
- Mary is relaxing well between contractions. She is finding them hard but copes with them as long as her back is gently stroked with featherlike touches.

- Mary is lying in the bath having a cup of tea. She is finding this very relaxing and soothing.

Vaginal examinations should be written down as and when they are done. It is a good idea to write them in a contrasting colour ink.

You will need several pages for the labour as it unfolds. After the delivery of the baby, it is best to jot down events and recordings as they happen.

- Placenta delivered spontaneously into bedpan.
- Blood loss 400 ml.
- Baby suckled at the breast.
- Mary moved to the bed as she feels shaky.
- Baby Thomas; 7 lb 3 oz; Temp 36·8°C; Head circumference 35 cm; Length 55 cm
- 18:45 Mary is having a bath.
- 19:00 Mary has been to the lavatory to pass urine.
- 19:10 Mary is back in bed suckling the baby.
- Baby Thomas has been held by Clifford, by his big brother, by his Grandpa and by Joan from next door. He is alert, bright, warm and a good colour.

Then begins the postnatal record. On the day the baby is born, you will need to make two visits. Obviously if the baby was born at 11:30 p.m., you do not need to visit again that day. But if she was born at 10 a.m., you will need to visit again during the afternoon (you may still be there anyway, just celebrating). It is very comforting if you visit late in the evening to settle your friend in bed for the night.

Our code of practice states that: 'In domiciliary practice the midwife should visit to undertake detailed assessment of maternal progress, morning and evening for the first few days after delivery and then at least daily. On each occasion she must record her findings and observations entering the time, date and full signature in the woman's records.' Most midwives interpret this as being two visits for the first three days, then daily until the tenth day, and then, after that, occasional visits until day 28.

The statutory duty of the midwife after she has delivered a baby is to send notification of the birth to the supervisor of midwives for that area. She can obtain a birth notification form from the supervisor of midwives or from the district health authority.

Every day it is usual to check your friend's physical condition. Many midwives take the woman's temperature, pulse and blood pressure (occasionally), examine her breasts, feel her fundus, examine her perineum and lochia, ascertain that she has no signs of thrombosis in her legs, and find out if she is passing urine normally and whether her bowels are functioning well. This physical examination is, of course, important but even more important is the time spent talking with the woman about how she feels about being a mother and about this baby, and giving practical help — such as topping and tailing the baby each morning, helping with dressing the toddler while you chat to your friend and by always making a cup of tea for her when you arrive. (I remember delivering a friend just at the end of my holiday so that I was back at work on day 2. From then on I would arrive at 6 a.m. to do my postnatal visit. I had a front door key, and made a cup of tea for my friend and her husband so that the rude awakening at the crack of dawn might not be too awful! It was so lovely to go into a sleeping household, so quiet and peaceful, and to go into the bedroom where the new parents were snuggled up in bed together. Often it was difficult to see baby Martha because she would be snuggled up in bed with them too.)

As a midwife we are privy to many intimate moments in a family's life. We are like beloved friends in people's homes when we are providing care to people we know. It is an honour to be welcomed in people's homes in a way that perhaps no one else is lucky enough to experience.

In the first ten days during which you visit your friend and her baby, you will have helped to establish breastfeeding, and taught her how to change a nappy, how to wash the baby's hands, face and bottom, how to bath the baby and how to be as organised as possible about baby care. Now it is probably time to taper off your visits — a visit on the twelfth or thirteenth day, another on the sixteenth, perhaps the twenty-second and so on until you discharge her to the care of the health visitor at 28 days. Hopefully the baby will have regained her birth weight by then. (Scales to weigh babies can be bought at anglers' shops. They hang the baby from your hands and are usually accurate. You can also use ordinary kitchen scales with a large plastic mixing bowl for the baby to lie in.)

At the time of delivery of the baby, it is a good idea to let the supervisor of midwives know how the delivery has gone, and it is polite to let her know when you have discharged your friend.

DOCTORS

One of the greatest dilemmas for midwives at the moment is the referral of a woman to a doctor for a further opinion, but it is much better to do it straight away and get it sorted out so that the woman can come back to your care.

For many midwives used to working in a hospital, the attitude of the general practitioner is extremely refreshing. Because they are working in the community, seeing people all through their lives, their view of humanity is healthy and wide, and they are not so oriented to pathology as their hospital counterparts. Even if they are not prepared or not able to support you through the actual home confinement, they will invariably be willing to prescribe for thrush or cystitis. They will usually be willing to take and send blood samples to the local haematology department. They will also usually be willing to come out and suture the woman following the delivery if it is a skill you do not have. They, above all others, understand the philosophy of independent midwifery because they have managed to retain a large degree of independence while working within the National Health Service. They can be enormously supportive if you are lucky enough to find one or two to whom you can go.

Hospital doctors can be very helpful if you can get to know them and gain their respect, but it is worth remembering that at this time only a tiny handful of doctors practising hospital obstetrics have ever seen a home delivery — I am probably talking here about your oldest consultant obstetrician. Most have no idea what it involves.

Some of the doctors working in hospital will have gone out on 'flying squad' calls. They will have been frightened. Their senses will have been heightened because of the anxiety they were feeling. They will have seen themselves (and been seen) as the 'saviours' of the situation. Furthermore, whatever the situation was — a woman having a postpartum haemorrhage three days after hospital delivery or a woman miscarrying at

20 weeks — they will think of this highly abnormal situation as 'birth at home'. The equipment they used may have been highly unsuitable for domiciliary practice as it was packed and planned by people who have never practised in someone's bedroom but only in a vast delivery room. The range of equipment may be enormous, but still no one can find a catheter. This sort of experience colours the hospital doctor's feelings about home birth.

The hospital doctor has been told repeatedly, since he or she was 18, that home births are dangerous and belong to another age. Appendicectomies are no longer performed on kitchen tables and births should not take place at home. The fact that two more dissimilar things would be hard to find and that there is increasing evidence that birth at home is possibly *safer* for low-risk women seems not to have been recognised. The philosophy in most maternity units is that birth is only normal in retrospect, that being born is the most dangerous period of a person's life, that the role of the obstetrician is to 'save' the lives of babies who are in danger from their mothers' bodies.

To learn about the progress of labour and to become acquainted with the feelings generated by a woman going through a normal labour, we need to be with women and experience many labours from start to finish. Student midwives have trouble managing to see complete labours during their training, but because the intention for them to do so is there, it is more likely that they will actually stay with a woman throughout her labour. For a medical student who spends only about seven days on a labour ward, during which time he or she is often called away to see breech, forceps and caesarean deliveries, the amount of normal labour seen is minimal. The next time he or she will work on a labour ward will be as an SHO. Six months later, still not having seen normal labour, the doctor is a registrar, an expert in abnormal labour and very necessary, but lacking the experience of the doctor who trained 25 years ago — of going out with the community midwife and being with women going through normal labours at home.

It can be harmful for a woman at this time of heightened sensitivity to be cared for by someone who is frightened of childbirth. The fear that she can so easily pick up from a referral to a hospital doctor can affect her self-confidence, her feeling of well-being, her joy in her pregnancy and her forthcoming birth.

Having acknowledged the disadvantage of hospital referral, it is important to acknowledge that it is sometimes unavoidable. In that case it is probably better to get it over and done with, rather than trying to treat something yourself, getting more and more anxious and ending up by having the same effect on your friend as you are trying to avoid by postponing referral. It will help your friend and your own credibility if you can go with her to her appointment. You should introduce yourself, explain why you are referring her, and behave in an efficient and professional way. This helps you enormously if you have to refer your friend again, especially in the event of having to refer her during labour. The doctors on duty will be expecting you. Your friend's wishes will be treated with respect and you will also be known and respected.

Damstra Wijmenga's study shows that when women chose between a home birth, delivery and a 24-hour stay in hospital, or delivery and a seven-day stay in hospital, they had less intervention if they opted for a home confinement or for the shorter stay in hospital. It would also appear from his work that, if the woman's wishes for her labour are known, it will affect the treatment which is given to her in labour. I am sure we have all seen this in practice. When a woman has expressed very definitely her preference for a certain type of delivery but it cannot be achieved, the midwives and doctors are influenced by her wishes and do their best to try to make whatever is happening as like the original desires as possible. For instance, if a woman who wanted the baby delivered onto her abdomen has to have a forceps delivery, often the obstetrician doing the delivery will very gently deliver the baby onto her mother's abdomen. Alternatively, the obstetrician might rotate the baby's head with forceps so that the woman can push the baby out herself.

If the woman was originally booked for a home delivery or expressed repeated desires for a home birth, the midwives will try to make the delivery ward as home-like as possible. There will be fewer interruptions. Staff will try to keep out of the room so that the woman and her partner are not disturbed. Sensitive doctors will knock gently at the door and will wait for the midwife inside to come to talk to them. The atmosphere will be more peaceful than usual.

The presence of an independently practising midwife also seems to have an effect on the doctors and the hospital midwives. Everyone strives to show the woman and the midwife that it can be done just as gently within the hospital. So if your friend has to be referred to hospital during labour, your presence and good prior relations with the doctors will make a big difference to how the delivery unfolds, and you can take heart that it will probably be conducted more sensitively than it might have been.

One final point about referrals — remember always that you are referring your friend for a professional opinion, for a consultation. Once that consultation has been sought, it is up to your friend whether or not she accepts that advice. Once the illness or abnormality has been dealt with, the woman can be regarded as 'normal' again and you can resume care of her.

Some women would like an ultrasound scan. Your supervisor of midwives will arrange this. Again, it is better if you can go with your friend. She may be bombarded with questions and comments — 'Haven't you seen a consultant, just in case?', 'Well, you're either brave or mad', 'You should have a referral from your GP', 'Home deliveries aren't allowed any more. Do you think you might be prosecuted?'.

Pregnant women are very soft and impressionable. They need gentle and sensitive treatment. The stories they hear from insensitive and uncaring lips could give them nightmares and make them anxious. If they need to be seen in a hospital, they need someone with them who is feeling strong and *who knows that what they are doing is perfectly reasonable, within the law, and safe*. Usually the best person to do that is their midwife.

PREPARATION FOR BIRTH AT HOME

If you are lucky, the supervisor of midwives may lend you the equipment you need. For some years my own supervisor of midwives would lend me:

- A delivery pack.
- A suture pack.
- Suture material.

- Syntometrine and syringes.
- A mucus extractor.
- Local anaesthetic and syringes.

It is worth collecting the equipment you need slowly over the years. There are several medical suppliers who can supply by post (see Appendix 5). If you go to see them, it is often better to telephone first so that they can get the equipment ready for you.

When I started midwifery, I was given a sphygmomanometer, stethoscope and Pinard's stethoscope for Christmas. Over the years I have bought the following basic equipment.

- Sphygmomanometer (a small portable one is best and cheapest).
- Stethoscope.
- Pinard's stethoscope.
- A receiver or stainless steel bowl (which can be boiled).
- Plain dissecting forceps.
- Two large Spencer Wells artery forceps.
- Scissors.
- A suture holder.
- Mucous extractor (two).
- Inco pads (lots) or clean old towels.
- Syringes and needles.
- Syntometrine and/or ergometrine.
- Cotton wool.
- Urine testing sticks.
- Sanitary towels.

There is some additional equipment that it is good to have. It can usually be borrowed from your supervisor.

- Baby resuscitation bag.
- Neonatal laryngoscope.
- Intravenous giving set and infusion. Haemacel is a plasma substitute and has a shelf-life of eight years. It is useful for increasing blood volume in the unlikely event of excessive bleeding.
- A small heating pad.
- Entonox machine and cylinders.

As soon as possible after booking your friend, you need to give her a list of things to get ready for the birth and, later on at about 34 weeks, you need to check that all the things are ready and together in one convenient place. They can all be put in a large cardboard box or on a table or other flat surface.

Here is a list I give to the women I am going to deliver:

Please have the following ready for your birth day

- A flat surface.
- Two kitchen rolls.
- Newspapers.
- Two dustbin liners.
- Ten bin liners.
- A bucket.
- A washing-up bowl.
- Two paste jars or jam jars.
- One low reading thermometer.
- One ordinary thermometer.
- Bottle of Savlon or Dettol.
- Bottle of surgical spirits.
- Clean old sheet or towel to wrap the baby in.
- Two old towels for sitting on.
- A measuring jug.
- Soap on a saucer.
- Flannel.
- Three towels (for mum, midwife and baby).
- Sanitary towels (lots).
- Cotton wool.
- Clothes for baby.
- A sheet of brown paper.
- Hot water bottle.
- Three packets of inco pads (order from chemist).
- A large saucepan.
- A new nail brush.
- A tea towel which has been boiled for five minutes and when dry has been ironed with a very hot iron and then put in a new polythene bag.

THE DELIVERY AT HOME

It is reassuring for both you and your friend if you telephone her every morning from about 37 weeks on. You can say hello and find out how she is feeling. She can find out where you will be that day.

I recall with great pleasure a friend I delivered. On the Monday I told her where I was going to be each day and evening that week. I told her that on Thursday I would be having an evening at home.

She went into labour on Tuesday morning and had a baby boy. On Tuesday evening she said to me, 'We have booked you and your husband in at X Restaurant for 8 p.m. on Thursday evening, and you are to go and eat and drink what you like. It's a present from us'. That evening was like magic. We wafted into this beautiful restaurant, were ushered to our seats like royalty and were really well looked after. We had the most wonderful meal and then wafted out again — a memory we both treasure.

Having telephoned your friend regularly so that she knows where you are at all times (this is not so necessary if you carry a bleep — several firms including British Telecom provide them) one day she will ring you and say that she thinks this is *it*. It is important to have everything ready well in advance for this birth, so that by the time your friend is 36 weeks pregnant, you can go at a moment's notice — picking up your fully packed bag as you go.

As you leave your house or, more likely, your warm bed, you will feel very frightened and alone. Because of the conditioning of our training and experience, we have learnt to feel fear when confronted with a birth, but this is an inappropriate emotion at this time. Do not worry — you are about to learn other more comfortable emotions about childbirth — you are about to learn to trust women's bodies.

You get to your friend's house (if it is night-time, suggest to whoever rings you that they leave lots of lights on at the front of the house so that you can find it easily). Once you are inside the front door, you will sense the lovely feelings of excitement that are filling the house. Absorb the feelings for a minute, and then go to say hello to your friend. Just look at her and absorb how she is, how she is feeling, and the sort of feelings she is giving off.

Get one of the people who is there to help by filling the large saucepan three-quarters full with hot water. Place in it your receiver, two large artery forceps, a pair of scissors, and the small bowl or cup your friend got ready. These need to be covered by the water and they need to boil for 20 minutes before being turned off and left in the boiled water until they have cooled down a bit.

The next step to take is to thoroughly examine your friend. Ask her when everything started, how it started and what is happening now. Take her temperature, pulse and blood pressure. Test her urine and palpate her abdomen. Ascertain the position the baby is in and whether or not the head is engaged. Listen for the baby's heartbeat, and observe it for regularity and pace. It is very useful to draw a small cross on your friend's abdomen immediately over where the fetal heart is heard at its strongest so that it is easy to find next time, and also so that it is easy to find it when she takes up different positions. These crosses make a lovely record of the descent of the baby as the fetal heart traces a path down the abdomen.

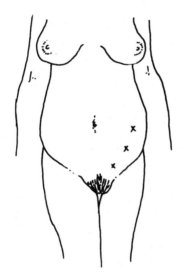

If you want to do a vaginal examination, get your friend to go and wash her pubic area thoroughly with one of the clean flannels she has got ready. Wash your own hands and dry them on the clean towel that your friend has got ready for you. Put on your sterile gloves, gently insert your index and second fingers and gently examine —

The vulva and vagina. Are they warm and moist and normal?

The cervix — Where is it? Is it anterior so that you can feel it immediately? Is it central so that you can find it quite soon? Or is it posterior so that it takes ages to find and sometimes is so far behind the baby's head that you cannot actually feel it?

The cervix — How does it feel? Is it long and thick? Or is it thinning and is less than a centimetre thick? Is it soft and loose or is it well applied to the baby's head?

The cervix — Is it dilated? How much?

The membranes — Are they intact? Bulging? None felt?

Liquor — Is there any? If so what colour? Clear? Blood stained? Stale meconium stained (brown or khaki)? Fresh meconium stained (green)?

The baby's head — Where is it? Is it above the ischial spines so that when you try to feel it you can only reach it with the tips of your fingers?

Or is it at the spines so that your fingers are almost completely inside the vagina but there is little of the lower part of your fingers outside.

Or is it below the spines and almost immediately felt?

Having completed your vaginal examination, again check the baby's heartbeat.

The most important duty you have as a midwife is to observe and absorb the atmosphere around your friend. Sit yourself in a comfortable chair and, if you find it difficult to know what to do with your hands, take some knitting or sewing with you. You need to be relaxed and comfortable. When your friend or the person or people with her become anxious, the sight of you sitting there, relaxed and calm, will be an enormous source of strength for them. It will not be so easy to knit or sew if you make the room dark, but removing outside stimuli will help the labour to progress and will allow your friend to surrender to her labour and to go inside herself and tap the huge resources which are in-built for women in labour.

If you are relaxed and comfortable and aware of the atmosphere around you, you will also be aware when everything is progressing well and when it is not. You will tune into instincts you were not even aware that you had. Birth is primeval and genetically learned. You will be amazed at how much you know over and above your knowledge as a midwife.

Having said that you will pick up any problems just by instinct, it is still a good idea to listen to the baby's heartbeat regularly. But if the mother is calm and relaxed, it is very likely that the baby will be calm and relaxed too.

Other duties of the midwife during a labour at home are to make sure that the woman always keeps her bladder emptied and that she is kept well nourished with nourishing soups or drinks — lemon and honey, tea, herb teas with honey, home-made lemonade, anything she fancies. Her labour companions also need to be kept well nourished. Labour is very demanding and those present can feel very drained which then lowers the spirits. The midwife can ensure that everyone (including herself) is kept topped up.

As labour progresses, you will want to get ready a hot water bottle for warming the baby's clothes and the cloth to wrap the baby in when she is born. Then go and get your tray, clean it with surgical spirit or Savlon, and lay your boiled teatowel on it. On that put your receiver (which contains the large artery forceps and scissors) and your small bowl or cup. Cover all these sterilised instruments with the other end of the boiled teatowel. At the same time, put your stitch holder and plain dissecting forceps in to boil, but only put the heat on low otherwise it will boil dry.

When labour is progressing fast, fill the washing-up bowl with hot water, and take it, the soap on a saucer and your towel in to where your friend seems to be settled. With the bowl of water, you can keep your hands clean and ready for delivery, and you do not need to keep going away to wash them.

If you need to do a vaginal examination again and your friend no longer wants to go as far as the bathroom to wash her pubic area, the cup or small bowl can be filled with warm water and a few drops of Savlon or Dettol put into it to wash your friend down with. A bedpan of your own is a great boon. I use mine a great deal — to catch the liquor if I think that the membranes are about to rupture, as a bedpan if the woman does not want to go as far as the lavatory to pass urine. In many ways a bucket is just as good for squatting on when she is getting tired. The floor can be covered with newspapers and a sheet of brown paper. Inco pads are, as usual, the most enormous boon. With the use of them and the two old towels, there is no reason why there should be any mess at all after a home confinement.

I remember the injured tones of Mrs Harrop — the midwife who delivered our first baby — when my husband offered her clean sheets for 'afterwards'. She said emphatically, 'I make no mess, Mr Flint. We shan't need clean sheets'. She was right too. There was no mess afterwards at all. The bin liners your friend has collected for you are for rubbish as you go along. The dustbin liners are to collect it all together at the end and put next to the dustbin.

The placenta can be delivered using controlled cord traction following an injection of syntometrine if that is how you feel safest delivering it. But remember that you can just wait — do not give syntometrine (unless the woman is bleeding) and just wait. Wait while the baby begins to look around, stretch and yawn, and search for the nipple. Wait while the mother explores her child. Wait while the father gazes in ecstasy and delight at his new-born and his amazing wife. Wait while the baby suckles. Wait while the parents discuss the wonders of the experience they have just been through. Wait while one of the companions goes and makes a pot of tea. Wait while the baby suckles some more and then some more. Wait while your friend gets herself into a more comfortable position. Wait a little longer, and eventually a small gush of blood will signify separation, and the placenta will plop out, into the bucket or bedpan if you have managed to get it there in time.

Either now or once it has stopped pulsating, clamp and cut the umbilical cord. Take the placenta and measure the blood loss in the bathroom. If your friend is ready to have a bath, you could run it for her, but she may prefer a blanket-bath or a shower. It can take a long time for a placenta to come out on its own. It is usually out in under three hours. If you are getting at all anxious you can check your friend's pulse. If it speeds up, you are right to be anxious, but if it is within the limits of normal — all is well.

When it is appropriate, examine, measure and weigh the baby. If you decide to bath her, make sure that she is near her mother so that her mother can see and touch her baby. My mother, who had five children, always complained that you could never see your new-born baby because midwives always do things to the baby with their backs turned to the mother, so hiding the baby.

It is essential to fill in the Birth Notification Form immediately and to fill in your own birth register straight away as well. Otherwise it is very easy to forget about it and to get into a muddle when you need to show the register to a supervisor of midwives.

After the delivery and any suturing has been done, scrub all the instruments with the nail brush and soap, rinse them and then boil them up again for 20 minutes. They can then be returned to your bag sterilised and clean, not carrying any infection from one house to another.

Leave the notes (the exercise book) at your friend's house while you are visiting postnatally. Ask your friend to fill in her thoughts and feelings and to put in her comments on the baby's progress, writing from the other end of the book.

I once saw notes made up by some Australian independent midwives which were most impressive and had several sections for the woman herself to fill in. Some of the questions were:

Do you exercise? Please specify.

Do you feel that your sexual relationship has changed appreciably since you became pregnant?

Do you plan to breastfeed this baby? Any thoughts on how long for?

Have you had any opposition to giving birth at home? Please describe.

Please list the people you plan to invite to your birth, why you have invited them and what their specific tasks/roles will be, if applicable.

Your mother's obstetric history. How many children did your mother have? How many were born at home? Were there any caesarean deliveries? Any breeches? Any complications of pregnancy and birth? How many children did she breastfeed? Any difficulties? Did she take diethylstilboestrol while pregnant with you? What was her attitude towards birth? What does your mother remember about your birth?

Please share with us your thoughts and feelings about your previous birth experiences, any things done to you or your baby that you did not like, and anything you would like us to know about such things as stitches. Please tell us what you want done differently this time.

If your partner was with you at previous births or has been at other births, please ask him or her to write down feelings, thoughts, hopes and wishes.

Why do you want to have this baby at home? And partner?

What do you see as the duties or responsibilities of your midwives? And partner's response to this question.

There are some things which can go wrong without previous warning during labour and birth and after. If you are a low risk woman, the chances of unpredictable complications are low. However, if such complications should occur, you and your baby might be at greater risk because of being at home. There are risks involved with childbirth just as there are with driving a car, some of which will never be eradicated no matter what our technology. There are also risks in having your baby in a hospital. If you opt for the set of risks involved in birthing your baby at home you need to find out what they are and how they can be dealt with. This can be done by reading and/or talking to your midwives. Please share your feelings and thoughts on this aspect of home birth. Also partner.

How do you feel about transferring to hospital if complications arise? Partner?

Please add any further comments or thoughts that you think are relevant to your midwives. Partner?

The woman's part of her notes are interesting and very relevant. Together you can make a diary of the whole experience. You must keep this record because as the Midwives' Rules note: 'A midwife must not destroy or arrange for the destruction of official records made while she is in professional attendance on a case and required to keep by these rules; if she finds it impossible or inconvenient to preserve them she must transfer them to the local supervising authority or to her employing authority, and details of the transfer must be duly recorded.'

When your friend is safely delivered, you should inform the supervisor of midwives. When you have finished visiting your friend on a professional basis — and at least by the twenty-eighth day — you should write to the supervisor of midwives informing her that you have discharged your friend from your care and asking her to inform the local health visitors.

Having delivered your friend at home, the way childbirth *can be* will have been revealed to you. You will share a bond with that family that is close and warm. You will have learnt many things that cannot be learnt from books, and every time you go to that house in the future, you will recall how you felt that special time — how it felt when you came in through the door at four in the morning, what the atmosphere in the house was, the birth of that particular small person.

You will also have grown enormously in confidence — confidence in your skills as a midwife, confidence in the process of labour, confidence in women's bodies. To have been there will have been a privilege — as it should be at every birth we attend, but unfortunately it often does not feel like that because of the way in which we work.

References and Further Reading

Chamberlain, G., Gunn, P. (1986). Confidential enquiry into facilities in the place of birth. London: *National Birthday Trust.* 1986.

Damstra-Wijmenga, S. M. I. (1984). Home confinement: the positive results in Holland. *Journal of the Royal College of General Practitioners*; **34:** 425–30 (August).

Chapter Eleven

Stillborn and Handicapped Babies

Nothing can ever make delivering a stillborn or handicapped baby an easy task. At the end, no matter how well and sensitively you have done it, you will come out feeling drained, sad and depressed. But one thing is certain — it is good to feel that you have made the experience as positive for the parents as it is possible to do. By comforting them, you will receive comfort.

No one can plan ahead for their reactions to such a sad situation, but it is much easier to react in a way that is helpful to the parents if you have thought about it beforehand and have made some plans, even if they are sketchy ones.

When a baby dies in utero, it is a tragedy for the parents. This might seem a trite observation, but it is a tragedy even for parents who originally did not much want the baby. It is also a tragedy for a woman who knew she was carrying a baby with some type of handicap — and the grieving may seem even more intense just because the mother feels that she alone is grieving for this baby.

Where does the midwife come in? It may be she who originally cannot hear a fetal heartbeat during an antenatal consultation. It may be she who holds the woman's hand when the operator examines the uterus with ultrasound scan after fetal movements have not been felt for a period. It will be she who looks after the woman when she goes into spontaneous labour, or when labour is induced.

The woman needs to talk about the coming labour. She needs to know that it will be no different from any other labour, but that it will be most unusual for her to have to have any stitches after the birth because the baby's head will be slightly softer than usual and so the baby will slide out more easily. She needs to talk about the baby inside her. It will be helpful to point out to her that this baby is the same baby who was inside her yesterday, who was kicking about and sucking his thumb, and that this is exactly what the baby will look like — a baby, but a baby that is dead. Many women dread what is going to emerge from them. They need to hear you say that this is how the baby will look.

The woman approaching labour will be experiencing many 'if only' thoughts.

- If only I hadn't smoked, the baby might not have died.
- If only I hadn't missed my last appointment at the clinic.
- If only I had come here yesterday.
- If only it were yesterday.
- If only we hadn't made love, it might not have happened.
- If only I hadn't run for that bus.
- If only I could go to sleep, then perhaps I'll wake up and this will all have been a horrible dream.

The man is also desperately upset and frightened about what is going to emerge from his beloved's body. Many men are apprehensive about being with their partner during a normal labour. They are even more anxious about labour when they are anticipating some sort of monster to emerge. It is important for the midwife to repeat to the man what she has explained to the woman. In fact, there is no harm in repeating whatever you say to them both several times, because when people are in a state of shock, they do not hear what you are saying.

The labour will progress, often slowly, because the presenting part is not as firm as usual and does not stimulate cervical dilatation as well as the normal vertex.

The midwife needs to keep both parents well hydrated, with plenty of drinks and little snacks throughout their labour. She also needs to join in — both to keep herself feeling strong and so that they feel that she is with them and sharing the experience with them.

The midwife needs to give both parents a great deal of physical support — rubbing the father's back, stroking the woman's abdomen, arms and legs, putting an arm round either parent, caressing both parents.

The midwife will also need support herself. It is a great help to have another midwife with her — just to care about her and to help and observe. It might be a senior student midwife, but it needs to be someone who has volunteered and not someone who has been 'sent' in to help.

During the labour the midwife will be keeping an eye on all the usual measurements.

- The woman's physical and emotional state.
- Urine output.
- Temperature, pulse and blood pressure.
- Abdominal palpatation and descent of the presenting part.
- Cervical dilatation.
- Analgesia given and required.
- Contractions: strength, length and interval.
- Fluid intake.
- Milestones of labour.

All through the labour, the midwife is planning for the delivery of the baby and discussing it with the parents. In this way they are aware of what the midwife is planning and can say whether it is what they want or whether they would like something different.

From the work done by the Stillbirth Association, we have learnt that it is important for parents to see and hold their stillborn baby. Not all parents can cope with this thought though, so when delivering a stillborn baby it is important to allow parents to accept or refuse this opportunity. The time they have with their baby is very short so it is important that they can see the baby the whole time that it is with them, even if they cannot bring themselves to cuddle it.

The easiest way to help the parents to see the baby is to deliver the woman on an ordinary hospital bed as you will have more room than when the woman delivers on a conventional delivery bed. The way you receive their baby is important to the parents. If I know that the baby is going to be covered in meconium, I get ready a washing bowl and keep it filled with warm water so that I can clean the baby as soon as it is born. I also put a cord clamp on the delivery trolley so that when the baby is born, I can put on a small neat cord clamp rather than having a long cord hanging down with a pair of Spencer Wells artery forceps dangling from it. The other thing to prepare before the baby arrives is a cosy nest-like place where he or she can lie once born.

The great advantage of delivering on a larger bed is that the 'nest' — usually of soft towels — can be arranged on the end of the bed within full view of the parents.

The baby is being born. The dreadful thing about delivering a stillborn infant is the heavy and terrible silence. The parents wait with bated breath just in case there has been a mistake and the baby is alive after all, and then the sound of weeping fills the room.

Your weeping is not inappropriate. For the baby to be bathed in tears from its midwife is a fitting baptism for a baby who will never be christened.

The silence and the sobbing at the birth of a stillborn baby is almost unbearable. I find myself automatically talking to the baby — telling him or her how beautiful she is, how sad we are that she has not waited to meet us, how much her Mummy and Daddy were longing to get to know her. I do this while I am washing the baby and then putting her on the nest of towels. This is probably the best time for your midwife companion to take some photos of the baby. It is so very important for the parents to have a picture of their baby. Sometimes they do not want it immediately, but frequently they will ask for the photo a year or more later.

It is best to take a photo of the baby immediately after it is born and as soon as it is lying peacefully in its 'nest' because stillborn babies begin to look blotchy and purple very soon after birth. At this stage, however, they will look really beautiful.

It is quite a problem delivering the placenta of a woman who has had a stillborn baby. It is usually much softer than a normal placenta, and there is always the worry that the cord might snap with controlled cord traction. Often it is advisable not to give syntometrine and to wait for spontaneous expulsion of the placenta. If for some reason syntometrine is given, it might be as well to delay it until the baby has been settled in its little nest.

Once the placenta has been organised (either by the decision to wait for it to emerge or by the administration of syntometrine and controlled cord traction), the parents can be helped to cuddle the baby if they want to. Sometimes it can be helpful to them if the midwife suggests that she will cuddle the baby next to them and then, if they want to, they can cuddle it. Seeing the midwife cuddling their baby in a normal-looking way can help the mother or the father to say 'Yes, I'll hold him now'.

From the work of Phillipa Gunn and Mary Mulkerrins, we know that many parents are very upset that they never took up the midwife's suggestion that they hold their baby. It is essential that we are aware that time for these parents is terribly short. Phillipa Gunn suggests that, although parents must be able to refuse 'easily', it is often better to err on the side of encouragement by saying such things as 'Many mothers have really valued holding their baby', 'Shall I hold him next to you and then you might feel like holding him after a while', and 'Sometimes mothers change their mind about holding their babies so I'll mention it again after I've washed you'.

The same applies to babies with any kind of abnormality. If their parents have not seen what exactly is the matter with their baby, the dreams and nightmares that they have of their baby will be very vivid and frightening. If the baby has a deformity, it is often helpful to keep the baby's abnormalities covered up and to gently explore the baby together. You can reveal the abnormality very gently and slowly so that the parents have seen the worst — because whatever the worst is, it is never as grotesque as what the imagination of the human mind can conjure up.

Some parents like their baby to be dressed in his or her own clothes. Somehow it seems appropriate to dress them in something warm and soft. Some parents may be comforted by having a priest saying some prayers with them over their dead baby, and many hospital chaplains manage to provide very beautiful and relevant prayers for this sad occasion.

The tragic part of parenting a stillborn baby is that the contact with the baby is for such a short time. The midwife can help to prolong the time the parents have with their baby so that they have the longest time possible.

The more they can do with their baby, the more memories they will have of the short time they had with their child. This can be —

- Cuddling the baby.
- Dressing the baby or watching the baby being dressed.
- Talking to the baby.
- Arranging the baby in the receptacle ready to go to the mortuary.
- Putting a few fresh flowers around the baby.
- Putting one of the baby's toys in with him.
- Taking further photos of the baby.

Some hospitals have small Moses baskets in which the baby can be transferred to the mortuary. This seems warmer and cosier than a box.

Often grandparents, sisters and other relatives are relieved to see the baby and to have the opportunity to hold him or her as well. The parents can be given a cup of tea and the mother blanket-bathed. Then they can both be transferred to the postnatal ward if they are ready for their child to go over to the mortuary. Nowadays it is usual in any humane hospital for the father to be encouraged to stay with his partner, but often what he is given to sleep on leaves much to be desired. He often lies hunched at the foot of her bed in a camp bed which leaves him unrested and stiff in the morning. The best place for a grieving couple is snuggled together in a double bed. Grief causes real physical pain, and the pain of empty aching arms can only be assuaged by having those arms round another loving human being.

Both the parents and the grandparents and relatives will need to talk and talk about the baby, the labour, what the doctor said, what the midwife said, how the baby looked, why the baby might have died, what clothes the baby wore, what the baby's hands were like, who the baby resembled, what the baby's feet were like, how the baby looked. The mother needs to relive the birth and her time with her baby over and over again.

She will also need to go to see her baby in the chapel of rest before the funeral. Some mothers want to have the baby at home the night before the funeral so that he can at least spend one night in the nursery so lovingly prepared for him. The cruel part of this may be that the baby's coffin has by then been nailed down. The undertakers should be persuaded to leave the little coffin open.

It is essential for midwives to be very familiar with what happens at their hospital — who gives out the Stillbirth Certificate, what happens at funerals in their area, what chaplain they can call upon, whether there is a special social worker for parents of babies who have died and where the local representative of the Stillbirth Association can be contacted.

Women hate the thought of their baby being buried in the cold earth. They often want the baby dressed in woolly clothes in a vain attempt to keep the baby warmer.

The funeral is very sad and painful for all who attend. But it is important. It is a recognition that a person has died, and it is also a public goodbye which often helps the parents enormously. These parents will never experience birthday parties or exciting events with this child but at least they will have this important event to remember and think about.

The parents need to know where their baby is buried so that there is an identifiable place for their child. Some women go weekly for years and years to put flowers on the grave. Other women feel peaceful after the funeral and do not feel the need to go. Some just find it much too painful to go.

The midwife who delivered the baby will feel terribly disturbed and upset by the event, especially if she knew the parents before the birth. She too needs to talk through the birth-death as often as possible. Often she can do this with the parents which is mutually beneficial. Weeping together helps to wash away grief and to bring peace and acceptance.

The midwife also needs to talk it over with her colleagues. The more they go through it together, the more it will help all the midwives when they have to deliver a stillborn baby. The use of role play can be very helpful, but it should only be done in a very supportive and safe environment where people can feel safe to cry and are able to receive comfort from each other.

DELIVERY OF A HANDICAPPED BABY

In some ways the delivery of a handicapped baby can be more difficult than the delivery of a stillborn child because it is usually unexpected. So the midwife has not prepared herself or the parents, and she reacts spontaneously in ways that may not always be the most helpful to the parents.

There is one golden rule to remember when a baby is greatly handicapped — however gross the abnormality, it is not as bad as the monsters the woman will imagine if she has not seen the baby. I remember the pleasure in the voice of the mother who was describing her anencephalic baby — 'She was perfect up to her eyebrows'. The midwife may have a very deep desire to protect the parents from seeing a baby who looks awful to her, but the parents' minds will be put at rest when they know the full extent of the malformation, when they are told and shown the truth.

Parents who have a baby with a handicap will be in a state of severe shock. Often the degree of shock and grief may have nothing to do with the severity of the condition. I remember the total rejection for several days of a baby girl because she had extra digits on each hand. I also remember the loving and gentle nursing of a baby with very severe spina bifida by her parents as she gasped her way through the few short days of her life.

We can never know what each individual handicap means to another human being but we can see the grief of parents who have a baby with a handicap and how much they need to talk through their experience. The person usually best equipped to talk through the experience with the parents is the midwife who was with them at the delivery.

This midwife will also need to talk through her grief and shock. She too will be having vivid dreams of delivering monstrous babies. She too will need the opportunity to weep with someone who knows why she is weeping. The appropriate people would seem to be the parents of the baby.

The other obligation of the midwife who has delivered a handicapped baby is to put these parents in touch with other parents who have children who are similarly affected. In Appendix 5 I have included a list of all the voluntary groups I know of — you may know of others. Before the tragedy happens try to get to know who your local organiser is or who your local counsellor is.

No amount of sensitive imagining can help us to know what it is really like to have a child with a cleft palate, Down's syndrome or spina bifida. It is essential that we give the parents the opportunity to talk with someone who has trodden the same path. Another parent is less intimidating than we are in our uniforms or white coats. Another parent usually speaks in more 'normal' words, can reiterate and discuss what has been said to the parents and can help them discover what they really did not understand and what they really want spelt out. This is essential because parents in a state of shock really do not hear what we are saying and they need to hear the same thing said over and over again. They need the opportunity to mull over what was said and the implications for their future life.

The needs of parents with a handicapped baby are similar to the needs of all parents. They need to have the opportunity to gaze and gaze at their baby. They need to be encouraged to handle their baby, and they need the opportunity to talk and talk.

Perhaps a nicer term instead of 'handicapped' is 'challenged'. I remember a Down's teenager who asked her mother, 'Mum, what does being handicapped mean?', and her mother's answer — 'It just means having to try harder than everyone else, darling'.

MISCARRIAGES

At whatever stage a baby dies, it is a tragedy for its parents. When a woman experiences a miscarriage or the death and loss of a very pre-term baby, she will feel all the grief she would have experienced if the pregnancy had been further on. She needs to talk through her experience time after time, and often she will be helped in her anguish by being put in touch with a miscarriage support group. These are groups of women who have joined together to give each other support after miscarriages.

The other group of women who often feel great grief are those who have had a termination of pregnancy. They too have lost their baby and often their grief is even more poignant because they have lost their baby through their own volition. Often they find it almost impossible to confide in friends or close relatives because of the circumstances surrounding the termination. When women have had no chance to resolve their grief at a termination by talking and talking through it, the grief may reappear during subsequent pregnancies, either as increased anxiety for this pregnancy and this baby or as punitive feelings towards herself if she then has a spontaneous miscarriage.

When a woman has a miscarriage, it can be helpful to her to look at the fetus and examine it. This is not always possible but many fetuses are very beautiful, and this can help her to know what she is grieving for. It is also important to reassure a woman who has had a very painful miscarriage or premature labour and is expecting another baby that labour is usually much easier and less painful than a miscarriage. This is because emotionally the woman is not fighting against it and because the uterus has more to contract against and seems to work more smoothly.

The work of a midwife involves great joy and a sense of the miraculous. Much of our working life is spent on an emotional high point. Like all very vivid emotional experiences, being a midwife can also involve great tragedy and grief. For this reason alone, it is important that you have someone or some people who you can go to after these very sad experiences and talk and talk. People who can hug you when you cry, and people who care about you and how you feel. Have you set up your support group yet?

References and Further Reading

Gunn, P., Mulkerrins, M. (1985). The midwives' participation in the North West Thames Regional Health Authority confidential enquiry into perinatal deaths. *Research and the Midwife Conference Proceedings*. Available from Nursing Education Research Unit, King's College, London University.

Chapter Twelve

Breastfeeding

'The two lie close in each other's arms, dark eyes gazing into dark eyes, breaths soft and panting as the erect, hot tissue searches for the soft, moist, open orifice.'

What is this description of? Yes, it could be a description of lovemaking, but when I wrote it I was thinking of breastfeeding. I often feel that there are many similarities between the two processes.

In both instances, the woman releases the hormone oxytocin. In order to do this, women usually need privacy and peace. In both instances, naked flesh is against naked flesh, and a substance is flowing from one person's body into another person's body. In both instances, the mechanics of the operation improve with practice and may well be extremely awkward at first and even painful. This is the case even though they are both instinctive skills.

In the same way that there are some lovers who fall into each other's arms and make glorious, passionate and orgasmic love from the start, there are also some women who never experience any problems at all with breastfeeding. The baby comes out, looks around for his mother's nipple, latches on and begins to suckle and never looks back. This chapter is written not for them but for the great majority of women and their midwives for whom breastfeeding is a learned art, accompanied by a bit of blood, sweat and tears.

Breastfeeding is both an instinctive and a learned skill. I remember the white marble-like breasts of a woman breastfeeding her baby in the kitchen of our home when I was probably about two years old. That picture is indelibly etched on my mind — perhaps I have that woman to thank for my own happy experiences of breastfeeding my children. It is much more likely, however, that I have my own mother to thank for breastfeeding me and my siblings.

As Chloe Fisher (the midwife who has helped so many midwives to guide and support women through breastfeeding) says, women in 1986 have often never seen a baby breastfeeding and many women attempt to 'bottle feed' their babies with their breasts. It seems to me that one of our greatest contributions as midwives is to teach women about breastfeeding long before they actually attempt to do it.

It is no use me or any other midwife telling pregnant women about breastfeeding. For the pregnant woman, the labour itself is her big watershed. She can think no further than that. Furthermore, a pregnant woman's attention span and her ability to absorb information is reduced. When a midwife tells a woman about breastfeeding, information often falls on deaf ears. No matter how well the midwife presents the information, the woman will respond much better to her peers telling and showing her what breastfeeding is like.

So much of the work of the midwife is networking, getting women in touch with one another. How about a group of mothers breastfeeding in a corner of the antenatal clinic? Women badly need to see *how* it is done. How about a breastfeeding group on the postnatal wards every Tuesday and Thursday? How about saying to a woman — 'Oh, you live in Cliveden Road. Jane Simmonds lives at number 36 and she had a baby six months ago. I know she's still breastfeeding. I'll get her to invite you round and you can talk about feeding your baby'.

The more a woman can see babies breastfeeding, the more she can talk to women who are breastfeeding and the more friends she has who are breastfeeding, the easier it becomes for her to breastfeed. This I think could be our greatest contribution to increasing the number of women who breastfeed in this country — just helping women to get to know each other so that they can help each other to breastfeed. We should encourage the National Childbirth Trust, La Leche League and the Association of Breastfeeding Mothers into our hospitals and ask them for their help and expertise in setting up groups of breastfeeding women to befriend and encourage the newly delivered mother. Are we mature enough to let go? Do we care enough about women to give breastfeeding back to them? Can we take the trouble to help them to help themselves?

As midwives, there are several practical steps we can take to help a woman to breastfeed. First, we can examine a woman's nipples during pregnancy, and we can say encouraging things if the nipples are protruding. 'Oh, you've got lovely nipples for breastfeeding.' 'Excellent nipples — you'll be able to breastfeed very well.' 'What a lucky baby you've got. Your nipples were just made for breastfeeding.'

Most women need no nipple preparation at all during pregnancy, but if the woman's nipples do not protrude, she needs help in encouraging them to do so. She should be encouraged to roll her nipples gently between her thumb and forefinger frequently (probably daily), to stretch her areola to try to release the adhesions behind her nipple, and to encourage her lover to suck and play with her nipples during love play.

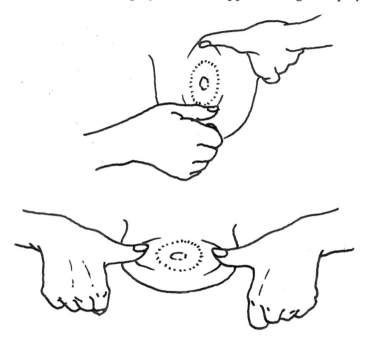

In research reported in 1978, E. M. Salariya showed that early initiation of breastfeeding (ten minutes after birth) had a significant effect on breastfeeding success. Here is an area in which midwives can have a significant effect on whether a mother succeeds with breastfeeding or not. If we take the third stage of labour to include the mother putting the baby to the breast, we shall have helped more women to breastfeed.

The way the putting to the breast is handled needs sensitivity. Women are shy about their breasts. They are often not happy for another woman to be handling them. If the woman can be left alone with the baby and her lover and with the words — 'I should let him have a go at sucking', they will invariably manage to help the baby to suckle. When the midwife returns, she can say with pleasure, 'I knew you'd be a natural at breastfeeding', and the mother will have gained enormous self-confidence from having been so clever as to have managed by herself.

E. M. Salariya also found that frequent suckling was enormously important in the establishment of lactation. In her report in *The Lancet* of November 25, 1978, she describes a regime of two hourly feeding until lactation was established which also made a significant difference to the length of time for which women breastfed. The sooner and more often a baby is put to the breast, the better.

Chloe Fisher always points out the importance of the position of the suckling baby. She also always points out how important unrestricted feeding is. As she observes in the *Midwives Chronicle* of February 1984, to time the length of a breastfeed is ridiculous and quite impossible. 'The number of minutes has always been strictly defined (except in 1979, when it was the number of seconds) yet no advice was ever given about the pauses. Should they be included or not? If included, then active feeding will be much shorter than the recommended time. If excluded, a mini computer would be required to estimate how much extra time should be allowed!'

In the same article is a graph which shows how 20 babies fed at different rates from their mother's breasts — one baby gobbled up 70 grams of milk in four minutes while at the other end of the scale, eight other babies took 22 minutes to take the same amount.

So how can a midwife help in the early days of breastfeeding?

By encouraging breastfeeding as soon as possible after delivery. If the mother is very tired or has had a caesarean, she can lie on her side and the baby can be helped to her breast while she dozes.

If the mother is very tired, it is likely she will have had a long gruelling labour with quite a large amount of analgesia. It is even more important for her baby to suckle while he is alert following delivery because he may become drowsy quite soon

because of the analgesia his mother has had. It may then be difficult to get him to suckle for several days following delivery, and it is important for his mother's peace of mind that she has already suckled him. After a long hard labour she may also be feeling disappointed about the whole experience. Having her baby suckling, even though she herself is dozing, may help the mother to come to terms with a less than happy memory of labour.

By encouraging frequent feeds of whatever length the baby decides on. If the baby is properly on the breast, it should not be sore. The whole nipple and a part of the areola need to be deep inside the baby's mouth. Many women experience a few seconds of pain when the baby begins to suck enthusiastically, but this should go away after about 10 to 20 seconds. This is a good time for her to practise her antenatal class breathing.

Most women who demand feed for as long as the baby wants and as often as the baby asks for it, find that their breasts do not get engorged or that the engorgement is minimal.

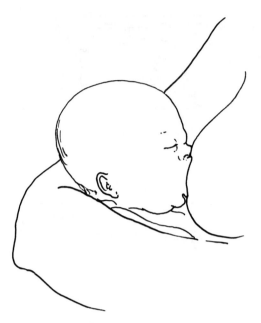

By not actively discouraging breastfeeding and by not actively encouraging bottlefeeding and undermining a woman's confidence in her ability to breastfeed. We, whose intention is to promote breastfeeding, are often guilty of actively promoting bottlefeeding. In the antenatal clinic, we hand out packets of free samples of bottle milk and rusks. We give women booklets which have advertisements for bottle milk on every other page. In the clinic, every advertisement for antenatal classes, every exhortation to stop smoking and every display of foods for healthy eating bears the legend *By Courtesy of Happy Milk Ltd.*

We label a new-born baby with labels marked 'Happy Milk Products'. On the cradle we pin a crib card marked —

Jason Merryweather
Normal Delivery
Wt 3·750 kg
Born 17/6/88
Time 08: hrs
HAPPY MILK FOR HAPPY BABIES

All these actions speak much louder than words, and what they really say to women is — *this hospital and the midwives in it think that Happy Milk is the very best milk you could give to your baby.*

We promote bottlefeeding even if we give a baby a bottle — whether it be a bottle of sterile water, dextrose or milk. No baby needs a bottle if she or he is breastfeeding. Bottles should not be in any postnatal ward which contains breastfeeding mothers. In fact, there is probably a very good argument for separating bottle and breastfeeders.

Babies will suck on almost anything, particularly the teat of a bottle which is elongated especially to press against the soft palate and so force the baby to suck. When the baby is given a bottle, she will suck. Even if she has just had a breastfeed which has lasted for three-quarters of an hour, she will suck. If the bottle were filled with fizzy lemonade, she would suck. What does this do to the mother? She has just given her child a huge feed, but her child is still hungry ('she must be — she is sucking'). This must mean that her milk supply is not adequate.

If the baby is a reluctant breastfeeder, giving her a bottle with one of those cunningly designed teats is even more damaging for the mother. 'She doesn't like my breasts, but she really loves the bottle. Look at how she's glugging it down.'

Even if it is only water that the baby is guzzling down, it is still hurtful to her mother. Furthermore, there will be the message printed on the label of the bottle of water — *Supplied to the Medical Profession by Happy Milk Ltd., Leaders in Infant Nutrition, Happy Milk for Happy Babies.* This message says loud and clear — We at St Hilda's recommend Happy Milk.

The insidious manner in which our postnatal wards are filled with bottles for babies should give us food for thought. Are babymilk manufacturers philanthropic organisations that they sell their bottles and teats to your hospital at below cost price? Why are they doing that? The answer is — to establish bottlefeeding among mothers and to make vast sums of money.

In *The Lancet* of May 21, 1983, Yves Bergevin *et al.* describe the effect of giving a packet of formula milk to alternate women as they left the hospital. Those women who had received a sample were more likely to have given up breastfeeding by one month than their counterparts who had not been given a milk sample. This second group went on breastfeeding for longer.

Giving a packet of formula milk to women seemed to undermine their confidence in their ability to breastfeed and deprived their babies of a long and complete period of breastfeeding.

As always the midwife's words have a huge effect on a woman's self-confidence. I remember a friend, who in the first unsure days after birth, lacking in confidence and feeling very inadequate, sat holding her baby and talking to her. A midwife walked into the ward, smiled at her, and said — 'you can see that you're a born mother'. My friend said that those few words lifted her spirit and buoyed her up for weeks afterwards. She was a born mother. It was recognisable to someone other than herself. It was recognisable to an expert.

You cannot tell every woman that she is a born mother because the effects of the words would become debased with over-use. But we can take every opportunity to congratulate and praise a woman's mothering skills. This will increase her self-confidence enormously.

- I love the way you talk to her. It's so good for her.
- He does love your milk, doesn't he?
- You do feed her well. You look so relaxed and good there.
- You can tell that you are used to babies. You are so proficient with handling them.
- I'm amazed that this is your first baby. You are so good with her, I thought it must be your second.
- He's listening to what you are saying. He loves you talking to him.
- You are managing very well.
- You are very good at mothering — she's a lucky little girl to have such a lovely mum.
- You handle him so caringly. It's beautiful to watch.
- She's feeding again, is she? It's obviously good stuff and she's enjoying it!
- Aren't you a lucky little boy to be getting such lovely milk?

Sixty-seven per cent of women in England and Wales start breastfeeding, but only twenty-seven per cent are still breast-feeding at the recommended four months, according to a DHSS survey carried out in 1980 by Jean Martin and Janet Monk. Most women give up breastfeeding because they feel that they have insufficient milk. But as we know that milk is supplied by demand — the more the baby sucks, the more milk is produced — so it seems strange that women feel that they have not enough milk. It might be worth exploring some aspects of breastfeeding and warning women about them in advance or during the early days of breastfeeding.

Breasts feel full and voluptuous during the early days of breastfeeding. Sometimes they leak. It is quite obvious to a woman that she is producing milk. Her baby sucks for half to three-quarters of an hour and looks sated at the end of a feed.

Women having second and subsequent babies often never experience the feelings of fullness. They have no engorgement. Their breasts do not leak or drip. They settle down to lactation very quickly and look unchanged. These women need to be warned about this because they often think that this indicates a lack of milk. In fact, it indicates that lactation has become established very quickly and smoothly. Women who demand feed completely their first baby often never experience engorgement. They may take this as a sign that their milk supply is lacking rather than what it really means — that they have got their milk supply organised very effectively.

Many women never experience dripping or leaking, and some women do not experience a feeling of 'let down' with some babies. Women need to know other mothers who are experienced in breastfeeding so that they can hear such information as they go along.

Many women have a crisis when their baby is about six or eight weeks old. By now the woman's breasts are back to their pre-pregnancy size so that they look and feel softer and floppier than during pregnancy and the early days of lactation. If women are not expecting this, it can make them anxious. Then the baby may have a day or two when he seems incredibly hungry and just wants to suck and suck all day and half the night. The woman fears this means that she has not enough milk. In fact, it is just the baby having a growth spurt and increasing his mother's milk supply by increasing his suckling. Within a day or two, her milk supply will have increased with his demand and all will be well — but she needs support and encouragement to get through this stage. Other women who have experienced the same thing are often the greatest help.

Another reason that women give up breastfeeding is that their babies reject the breast. Some babies are much more difficult to feed than others. Mothers need to be shown that they can breastfeed in many different positions and that this may help their baby to find it easier to fix on.

Women can breastfeed while standing up — this may make their breasts more acceptable to the baby who is rejecting them. They can also hold the baby under their arm so that the baby is suckling the breast at a different angle. Sometimes breastfeeding is about perseverance and the mother can be helped by women who have been through the same problems.

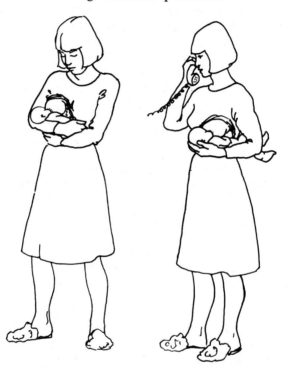

It is important for all women to know how to sterilise bottles and mix formula milk. It is essential that this should be demonstrated realistically — with a *real* kettle being used with real boiled water inside it, with really sterilised bottles and with the sort of teats women will use when they are in their own home. In many hospitals the equipment used for 'demonstrating' how to mix feeds is inappropriate and relies on women using their imagination. But when we are talking about something that may be outside a woman's previous experience and when we may be teaching women whose command of the language may be different to ours, no part of the demonstration should be left to chance.

It is midwives who can make or break a woman's resolve to breastfeed. It is we who are there at her most vulnerable times. The nutrition of babies in our community can be very much influenced by us. It is our responsibility. It is also our responsibility to give women somewhere to turn to. Here are some important 'somewheres', organisations which can help with breast feeding:

The National Childbirth Trust Breastfeeding Promotion Group,
9 Queensborough Terrace, London W2 3TB
Tel. 01–221 3822

La Leche League,
BM 3424, London WC1V 6XX
Tel. 01–404 5011

The Association of Breastfeeding Mothers,
131 Mayow Road, London SE26
Tel. 01–778 4769

References and Further Reading

Bergevin, Y., Dougherty, C., Kramer, M. S. (1983). Do infant formula samples shorten the duration of breast-feeding? *The Lancet*; 1(8334): 1148–51 (May 21)

Fisher, C. (1984). The initiation of breast feeding. *Midwives' Chronicle and Nursing Notes*; 97(1153): 39–41 (February).

Martin, J., Monk, J. (1980). *Infant Feeding 1980*. London: Office of Population Censuses and Surveys, Social Survey Division.

Raphael, D. (1976). *The Tender Gift: Breast Feeding*. New York: Schlocken Books.

Salariya, E. M., Easton, P. M., Cater, J. I. (1978). Duration of breastfeeding after early initiation and frequent feeding. *The Lancet*; 2(8100): 1141–3 (November 25).

Chapter Thirteen

Postnatal Care

The baby is born — the suturing is done — now the hard work begins.

For many new parents this is a time of immense shock. The time they have waited for, prepared for, dreamed of and longed for has come. Instead of the joy and exhilaration they were anticipating, there is just shock. For the woman, there is the shock that she still feels pain even though the labour is over — the soreness of a bruised perineum, the pain of uterine contractions. There is also the shock of motherhood. This feeling that she has been looking forward to for so long is just a feeling of overwhelming responsibility. 'Never, ever, as long as I live shall I be free again. I am tied to this person for ever and ever. Whatever happens to him, wherever he goes, he will always be tied to me. And now he depends upon me entirely, for his food, for his comfort, for his very existence.'

For both parents, there is the immense shock that this is a person. People expect babies. They do not expect a person and this baby is obviously a person, an *other*. Sometimes the person wins them over straight away. The person comes out and gazes with huge fascinated eyes at his parents. They are immediately entranced, under his spell, passionately in love with him.

More often the shock overcomes even the most enticing advances from this new person. The shock and the exhaustion are so overwhelming that the woman looks at her partner and says, 'You hold him. I just want to go to sleep. I just want to rest'. When she finally looks at the baby, what does she see? Someone ugly, someone mewling, someone hungry and demanding, someone she really could do without at this juncture in her life — and someone so foreign, so strange, so different, so *other*, that surely it couldn't have come from her. Surely this is some other baby, any old baby that the midwife has been and picked up from somewhere. Then she notices with a shock her lover's ears, big enough on a grown man, but grotesque on this tiny baby. Hopefully the baby may open his eyes and begin to cast his spell, but he may just lie there and mewl miserably as if he were as displeased with coming out as she is to have him out.

What about the other person in this family, the father? Soon he will probably be ushered out of the hospital. It is time to go

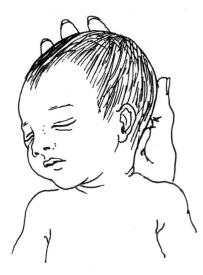

home, to ring the relatives, only the very closest at three o'clock in the morning. He will trudge home to his familiar flat, feeling bruised and dazed. He will let himself into the familiar smell of their home. There are the mugs they left this morning on the dresser, the towel left on the floor from when her waters broke, the familiar smell of the two of them, their place, their territory. In his solitude he realises that this has gone for ever, the halcyon days of peace and loving. The paradise of two lovers has gone never to return. The new life has started and he is shut out.

The most beautiful part of a home delivery is not the birth, not the familiarity of the surroundings, not the ability to move into whatever position the woman desires. The most beautiful part is when the midwife has gone and the lovers and their baby snuggle down in bed together — the new family, in their own place, in a bed that smells and feels familiar. The bed has in it two people who are familiar to each other, known and beloved. These two can gaze, inspect, look at, smell this new little person who is so unfamiliar, and they can do all this together. Not with one of them excluded and far away, but with both of them there starting this new stage in their lives together.

The woman in hospital now has yet another stress to go through — learning the intricacies of a postnatal ward. Has anyone told her that she must not get out of bed for four, six or eight hours (depending on the hospital), that no one is allowed to take baths before 9 a.m. because it upsets Doris the domestic, that babies are not allowed on the mothers' beds, that rest time is from 2–3 p.m., or even where the lavatory is?

Life in a postnatal ward is different from anything anyone has ever experienced before, unless you were sent at a very young age to a girls' boarding school. The behaviour expected of you there is not duplicated anywhere else. Women become disoriented and desperate in the postnatal ward — the noise, the bustle, the conflicting advice, the crying, the feelings of inadequacy and frustration, the things expected of them that they do not feel competent to do, the soreness of their nipples, the dirtiness of the lavatories, the lack of lavatory paper, gowns for the baby, of clean sheets and of ice for their water, the loneliness of being away from their lover. I have seen postnatal wards run efficiently by caring and sympathetic people. I have seen the excellent standard of care they have managed to give women. But I still see women in an alien environment, having to adjust to a situation which is not helpful to either the woman or her new relationship with her baby. Perhaps we should either send everyone home within minutes of the birth. Or perhaps we should have postnatal hotels where both parents can stay together and midwives are always on call in reception and keep popping in to lend a hand and check that all is well, but where the parents are in their room and food and refreshments are brought in to them.

The woman has to learn several skills during her time in hospital. In themselves they are not difficult, but because her perineum is sore, her breasts are heavy and leaking, and her insides feel as though they are falling out, she has great trouble getting these new skills sorted out in her mind. She needs to know how to change the baby's nappy, how to bath her and how to clean her face and how to feed her. Often the woman feels all fingers and thumbs and is made desperate by the speed and skilfulness of the midwives. What she needs is to be shown how her baby will look upon her.

Look back to your childhood and you will remember a time when you thought that everything your parents did was absolutely perfect and always right. You can reassure the woman that if every nappy she puts on falls off after 15 minutes, the baby will think — 'nappies are things which fall off after 15 minutes'. The baby will never think — 'my mother is cack-handed and can't put a nappy on properly'. The baby will not think like that until she is about 15 years old — until then mother is perfect and always right.

This was brought home to me strongly a couple of years ago when we went out as a family to a restaurant to celebrate my birthday. My intelligent and confident 16 year old daughter had a slight cold. She blew her nose, and then said to me very crossly, 'I wish you'd stop buying this flowery lavatory paper, Mum. It does embarrass me when I blow my nose'. To my surprise I saw that she was indeed blowing her nose on a piece of flowery lavatory paper. 'Well, why are you using lavatory paper?', I asked. 'Why don't you use a handkerchief or tissues?' She looked at me in amazement and said, 'But doesn't everyone use lavatory paper? I thought everyone used it for blowing noses on — you always had a roll in every room when we were little'. She was right. When my children were little, I kept a roll of toilet tissue in every room for small noses, and because her

Mum had done that, Becky thought that it was right, that this was what everyone used for noses. She was very cross when we all showed her the tissues or handkerchiefs that we were all using.

So for the child, the parent is perfect — knows everything, rules everywhere, is the source of all comfort, all nourishment, all love. The revelation of this small adorer in their midst is one of the great joys of parenthood. Even as children grow older, the fact that they like you so much is a great privilege and pleasure.

Some mothers find it difficult to feel affection for their baby. It may be that the birth was very traumatic and they feel violated. It may just be that the baby is difficult and not very happy to be here, constantly mewling and apparently rejecting advances of love and nourishment. It may be a baby of the wrong sex, or it may just be someone the mother does not instantly take to — a person she would not automatically like if she met them at a party. But, there are specific steps which will help the mother to grow to love her baby.

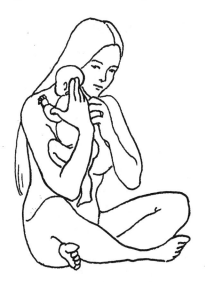

She should hold her as much as possible, especially naked, with bare skin against bare skin. She should gaze at the baby as much as she possibly can. She needs to get to know that little person's face, expressions, dimples, wrinkles. She needs to know that face as well as or better than she knows her own. She should smell the baby as much as possible so that the baby's smell becomes part of her memory and mind.

She should also talk to the baby for hours on end — telling her how she feels, what the world is like, where she lives, who her grandparents are, what the government has done recently, anything at all. Soon the baby will respond, will listen to her mother, will find pleasure in that voice and will eventually smile. The process of falling in love will start happening.

Babies have no sense of timing. They do not realise that when it is dark, civilised people go to sleep. They do not realise that when you have just been fed, you should not appear to be starving with hunger and ready and willing to start all over again. They do not realise that when you have just had your nappy changed, it is antisocial to then do so much poo that it squirts out of your nappy, runs down your leg and soils your babygro. Babies are used to a world where —

- They were cuddled all the time by the uterus.
- They were fed constantly by the placenta.
- They were never alone or apart.
- They were totally secure and often awake, especially in the dark.

Is it any wonder that some babies find it very hard to adjust to this new harsh world where they are often apart and on their own? They feel desperately lonely and abandoned sometimes. No wonder they cry and mourn the lovely place they used to know. Other babies, however, do not seem to mind. They are so nosy and so fascinated by this new world that they cannot stop gazing around, looking at every new colour, face and object — amazed that they have had the good fortune to end up here.

Because babies have no clock that tells them that night is different from day, the new parents are awakened probably two and often three times during each night. For the first couple of weeks, this is tolerable. But as they both become more and more exhausted, it becomes intolerable. To keep waking them up from sleep is a way of torturing them. Life becomes very very difficult indeed. They both need some sleep during the day. If they were working nights, which is what they are doing now, they would expect to go to sleep sometime during the day. Often it is the midwife who can point this out to the parents and who can encourage them to rest. It is sometimes an idea to give new parents a sheet with suggestions for the postnatal period. It could read something like this.

The first few weeks with a new baby

Congratulations on your new baby. He or she will bring you great joy and pleasure, and you will learn many new things from this experience. Having a new baby is like starting a new life or a new job which takes 24 hours a day. You will need someone to help you for at least two weeks after the birth and preferably longer. You will need to concentrate on the baby, feed her, change her nappies and talk to her. This will take up about 12 hours a day. It will not be from 8 a.m. to 8 p.m., and then you are off duty. It is half an hour here, two hours there, an hour and a half next. This will take up nearly all your time. You need someone to help by doing your washing, by cooking you nutritious meals, by shopping, and by keeping your home clean.

Having many visitors can be very hard on you. You will need to rest for at least two hours a day, and it is very awkward if visitors come when you are trying to catch up on some sleep. It might be an idea to have a day which is visitors day when the baby is very new. Have everyone to visit for one very demanding day and get it over with. It might be as well to say to anyone who plans to visit you that you hope they will bring a cooked dish or a cake with them. Try and cultivate a phrase to use when someone comes to the door — 'Oh how nice to see you. I've got half an hour before I plan to go and have a nap, and I'm dying for a cup of tea. Could you be a dear and go and make one for us both while I change the baby's nappy?'

People like to help and feel useful. It is not for you to rush round and make everyone luscious titbits when they come to visit you. That is for them to do for you. Try not to be too proud to let them help. You will feel so much better if you get as much rest as you possibly can.

The midwife will be visiting every day until the baby is ten days old and then once or twice more. If you have any worries or problems she can always be contacted by ringing this number _____. Please have ready each morning a hand towel which you keep for the midwife's use only, a clean set of baby clothes, a clean nappy, the baby's towel, some cotton wool, and a small bowl for washing the baby. Also please have a bin or wastepaper basket ready for the rubbish.

One of the greatest needs of the new parents is to talk through the birth over and over again. If the midwife can encourage this and can listen, she will learn a great deal about how the parents see her care and their baby's birth. If she does not have time to sit and listen, she can give them a form to fill in. It can be very open-ended and informal like the following questions.

Please write a description of your labour and the birth of your baby in your own words. (Midwife, leave lots of space here on the form.)

Please tell us what you specially liked about your treatment when you had your baby.

Please tell us what you specially did *not* like about your treatment when you had your baby and what we ought to change.

Please give this form to your Community Midwife when you have filled it in or post it direct to _____.

We need feedback from parents. Without it we cannot plan a service which caters for their needs.

Women, especially those who have worked until the birth of their baby, can experience extreme loneliness after the birth. It is immensely useful for them to get to know women having babies at the same time. This can be achieved in antenatal classes, by introducing women to each other during antenatal visits, by health visitors and midwives encouraging get-togethers among women, and by midwives encouraging support groups to develop. The National Childbirth Trust will have a branch or group in your area, and it is really worth getting to know them and asking them to take on women who need or who would appreciate their networks for postnatal women. It is also worth asking them if they could help with the setting up of groups within the health service. They have enormous expertise and ability and are generous with it.

Women need other women to talk with, to discuss their new life with. They need someone with whom they can discuss how strange they feel about this unfamiliar role. They need somewhere they can go to just to get out of the house. The new mother's life is not structured — she who is used to getting up at 7 a.m. so that she can leave the house at 7:45 a.m. to catch the train to get to work at 8:30 a.m., which she leaves at 12:30 to have her lunchbreak, which she finishes at 1:30. She then settles down to work until 4:45 p.m. when she leaves work to catch the train home.

It can be purgatory for many women when their day has no structure. You get up when you want to or when the baby wakes. You decide to go to the shops but then you can't because the baby is hungry and wants feeding *now*. By the time he has been fed and his nappy changed, it is 12:30 and it's early closing day and you yourself are starving. So you do yourself a sandwich and just as you raise it to your lips, the baby gives out a heart-rending cry of distress, his cry exactly pitched to cause the maximum emotional response from you.

Each baby's cry is different, has a different pitch, sound and length. Each baby's cry is geared specifically to its own mother's nerve endings so that she will respond to it immediately. Not only does she respond to this particular cry. She is made very uncomfortable by it. It makes the hairs along her back spring up. She can hear it when she is miles away from it. She is woken in the night when her body realises that it is going to start. She dreams about it. She finds it immensely disturbing and distressing, and she *has* to react to it.

The power a baby exerts over its mother is very frightening to many new mothers. If they love this baby, they treat the baby as a benevolent dictator. But if their feelings towards him or her are still very ambivalent, the demands the baby makes so stridently are almost intolerable. Having a baby was a mistake, the worst decision she has ever made. Who are the fools who said that she would enjoy it? Why was there this conspiracy of silence so that now she is trapped in this fiction of motherhood and loving babies? All she wants is out.

Women feel wicked and guilty for thinking these sort of thoughts. They know that there has never been another mother as unnatural, as unloving as they are.

They feel terribly sorry for their poor baby who has such an unsatisfactory mother. They feel a failure as a woman. Imagine their relief when they can go to a group and hear that other women feel and think the same as they do, when someone else dares to admit that there have been times when they have nearly thrown their baby out of the window because of its beastly crying.

It is essential that we make sure that women are in contact with other women, that they have an opportunity to meet other women who are at the same stage as they are. We must make sure that there is somewhere they can go to escape the four walls that seem to trap them. We have never fully utilised the postnatal check at six weeks after the birth. We think of it only as a physical check-up for the woman. It would be much more useful to make it a get-together for all the women who delivered that week.

One way of getting women together is this. They each write down their name, address and telephone number on four pieces of paper. Three of the pieces of paper they keep, and one they give to the midwives. While one midwife is asking the group how everything is going — how they are feeling as mothers, who is still feeling really distressed about their birth, who is finding it much harder than they had thought they would and so on — the other midwife is sorting through the addresses. She arranges them according to where the women live. She can then point out that there are three women who live in Stirling Road and another two in Windswept Way which is the next road to Stirling. She then tells everyone who lives near someone else about the other person, and then everyone goes round the room and asks another mother for one of her address cards so that they can get in touch later. Hopefully this will cement some friendships. It is also a great asset if hospital wards are divided into localities. For instance, in Shoreham Hospital they have Littlehampton Ward, Worthing Ward and Shoreham Ward. Women go to the ward of their own locality and often meet women who live a few roads away from them.

Women are shy. They don't naturally leap upon other women and say, 'I'm lonely. Are you? Can we be friends?'. It is up to us who have the sanctuary of our uniforms and our position to help women during this strange new time in their lives.

Many women feel depressed after they have had a baby. Often the depression is a combination of exhaustion and mourning the past — the past when they were carefree and had no responsibility, when their figure was perfect or at least better than it is now, when their lover was the principle person in their life and they were the principle person in his life. Now he comes home and goes straight to the baby and asks him how he is, whether he has had a good day, what the food has been like, what he thinks of the test match scores. It is the baby who is cuddled and petted.

Whenever anyone visits the new mother, the only person they want to see is the baby, the only person they want to hear about is the new baby. The mother can feel very second best. She is going through a huge transition, and it can take months before she has adjusted to her new life. It can also take months, even up to a year before she feels physically fit again. But usually with time, patience and the growing love she feels for her child, the woman will adjust to her new role, and her tiredness and depression will lift (especially once the baby starts sleeping through the night).

The depression mentioned here has to be distinguished from clinical depression. This needs treatment and referral to the GP who will then refer the woman to a psychiatrist. Severe postnatal depression makes the woman feel totally numb and dazed. She feels that she cannot cope with anything. All her movements are in slow motion, and it takes an inordinate length of time for her to manage even the simplest of tasks. It is a horrible disease and we are still a long way from identifying its cause. It seems to strike unlikely candidates as frequently as those who have suffered from psychiatric disorders in the past.

How can we help parents to adjust to their tremendous new role? How can we help fathers who often feel left out in the cold? I remember a father of a three month old baby saying to me bitterly, 'Every evening I go home from work, tired, hungry and waiting to see them. What do I find when I get there? It's a tip, there's no supper and it feels like a love-nest. The two of them have been playing and enjoying themselves all day. It used to be our love-nest, but now it's their love-nest. They're too busy even to welcome me. He's always feeding or crying when I get in, and he needs things doing to him all evening. All Marjorie can say is that she's tired — how does she think I feel?'

Brian Jackson wrote about the feelings of fathers in his lovely book *Fatherhood*. It is still a very unexplored area. We need to explore it further, so that we can help and support more.

How can we as midwives help women in their transition to motherhood? In many ways this is much more clear cut because we know more about their needs. We can —

- Help them to get to know other women in the same situation.
- Paint a realistic picture about how tired they will get.
- Encourage women to organise help for after the baby is born.
- Encourage women to walk somewhere every day after the baby is born. Physical exercise seems to help lift depression.
- Give women the opportunity to talk through their labours time and time again.
- Encourage women with our words. 'You do look after your baby well.' 'Doesn't he love your milk. You breastfeed him so beautifully.' 'Aren't you a lucky little girl, having such a lovely Mum?' 'I love to hear you talk to him so much. That's why he's so alert and bright. He's waiting for another chat.' 'You are such a good mother.' 'You're a born mother, you know.' 'Have you always wanted a baby?' 'You do it to the manner born.' 'I look upon you as a shining example of caring motherhood.' 'Well done, she looks so well and cared for.'

Our words as always have a dynamic effect. We can inspire and give confidence to a woman. The words we glibly say will be remembered for ever. We can help a woman, who is falteringly trying to come to terms with motherhood, to blossom into a mother filled with confidence and love for her child. We have an effect on the emotional health of our whole community. Midwives matter — they matter so very much to women. It's a great responsibility. Have you set up your support group yet?

References and Further Reading

Jackson, B. (1984). *Fatherhood*. London: George Allen & Unwin Ltd.

Chapter Fourteen

Supervision of Midwives

If you are unhappy about the conduct of your solicitor, you complain to the Law Society. If you are unhappy about the conduct of your doctor, you complain to the General Medical Council. If you are unhappy about the conduct of your architect, you complain to the Royal Institute of British Architects. If you are unhappy about the conduct of your midwife, you complain to the National Board. But, alone among all professions, midwives have someone else who can intervene in the relationship between professional and client — the supervisor of midwives.

The client may be more than happy with the conduct of the midwife. The baby may be alive and well. The midwife may feel that she has given the best care possible, but her notes can be scrutinised and the supervisor of midwives can criticise actions taken or not taken, decisions made or deferred, treatment given or not given.

Supervisors of midwives see themselves as wise experienced sages to whom other less experienced midwives come for advice and guidance. In 1937 a circular for the guidance of local supervising authorities was sent out describing the role of the supervisor of midwives. It said that they 'should be regarded as the counsellor and friend of the midwives, rather than the relentless critic, and should be one who is ready to instruct the midwives in the various points of difficulty which arise from time to time in connection with their work and make them feel that there is always someone to whom they can look for sympathetic understanding of the laborious nature of their profession'.

This can be enormously helpful to the midwife — to have someone more experienced and who cares about the midwifery profession and mothers, who can advise, encourage, teach and reminisce, who can be a role model, and who can be the older and wiser friend. This set-up works very well when the supervisor of midwives has kept up to date with clinical practice and thinking within the profession.

The 1937 circular, which was issued at a time when not all supervisors were midwives, says: 'The Departmental Committee on Midwives, which reported in 1929, pointed out that the inspection of midwives by a person without adequate experience of practical midwifery has a bad psychological effect upon the midwife, and reacts unfavourably on her methods of practice, as she is deprived of the opportunity for guidance on professional matters affecting the well-being of her patients.'

Supervisors see themselves as protecting the safety of the public. Their authority is given to them by local supervising authorities, which at the time of writing are the regional health authorities in England, the area health authorities in Wales, the health boards in Scotland and the health and social services boards in Northern Ireland.

Each local supervising authority exercises general supervision over all midwives practising within its area, and it usually delegates this responsibility to someone working nearer to the midwives. Usually the supervision of midwives is delegated to the senior midwife in the district, such as the director of midwifery services. Often there is more than one supervisor and a unit can have three or four, for example, the community midwives' senior midwife, the senior tutor and the labour ward senior midwife.

The fact that midwives work within a hierarchical structure and mete out punishment in a hierarchical structure means that often they do not understand any other way of dealing with their staff, and the functions of the supervisor may become entangled with those of employer and manager.

Supervision is not hierarchical. There is not a 'chief' supervisor. There are just supervisors. There should be a supervisor available for midwives to contact at all times. If a supervisor is away on holiday, it is no good her assistant saying that she will stand in as a supervisor. She cannot. It has to be someone who has been appointed by the local supervising authority and who has attended a supervisors' induction course not more than three years prior to their appointment. If no one within the unit is a supervisor, then the supervisor in the next district has to be asked to stand in.

To understand how supervision should work, let us look at how the supervisor reacts to the independent midwife. The independent midwife is not an employee of the health authority.

The supervisor does not have over the independent midwife the sort of authority which she might have over a midwife in the employment of the health authority. For example, she cannot exercise over her any powers she may have under the health authority's disciplinary procedure as distinct from those laid down by the act and the rules as given to the supervisor by virtue of her appointment as supervisor. For instance, the supervisor cannot tell the midwife what forms are to be filled in apart from the Birth Notification. She cannot say how many seconds following delivery the cord must be cut. She is there simply to guide and support the midwife in her practice and to protect the public.

When an independent midwife writes to the local supervisor of midwives informing her that she intends to deliver Mrs Pearson who lives in her area and asks her to send her an intention to practise form, she has in fact informed the supervisor of her wish to practise. The filling in of the form is necessary to enable the supervisor to inform her local supervising authority of the midwives who are practising in her area and of their credentials.

The supervisor, especially if she knows the midwife, usually just sends the notice of intention to practise form and a pleasant letter to say something like — 'It was good to hear from you. I hope Mrs Pearson's delivery goes well. Please don't hesitate to get in touch at any time'.

Often the supervisor will send the intention to practise form and will ask the midwife to come to see her and to bring her equipment and records with her when she comes. If the midwife intends to work from her own house, the supervisor may come to the house to inspect those parts of the house which are being used for professional practice. She will *only* inspect those parts of the house used in connection with the midwife's practice, so the doors of the teenagers' bedrooms can be left shut! But the supervisor will want to see the midwife's equipment, her records and her arrangements for storage of drugs. She may specifically ask to see the midwife's equipment for the resuscitation of the baby. The midwife should not get flustered about this. Remember that, in a survey carried out by the National Birthday Trust in 1985, one-third of community midwives attending home deliveries did not have either intravenous giving sets and/or fluids or a neonatal laryngoscope and intubation tubes. So their supervisors of midwives obviously did not feel that these things were mandatory for a home birth.

If a midwife practising independently is taking her equipment to the supervisor's office, she should take the case notes (or exercise book) of the woman she is delivering, and her register. If she does not have a register, she should ask the supervisor for one or obtain one from Hymns Ancient and Modern.

Most supervisors are supportive and encouraging to independent midwives. If there is anything that the midwife is having problems obtaining, the supervisor may get it for her. Some supervisors will lend Entonox equipment. If the woman would like or needs an ultrasound scan, the supervisor may be able to arrange this for her through the hospital. The supervisor will advise as to whether the midwife should buy or borrow any equipment that she does not have. She will also probably let the midwife know that she is there to help if she is ever anxious. Most supervisors see independent midwives as providing great hope for our profession, and they respect them for that. In at least one health authority, the supervisor of midwives arranges for all the independent midwives working in her area to have honorary contracts with the hospital, so that they can bring their patients into the hospital and look after them there if they need to. She also invites them to all midwives' study days. It is always wise to keep the supervisor informed of the progress of the woman you are going to deliver. If a supervisor is looked upon as the wise sage, she usually fulfils that role and is happy so to do.

It is the tragedy of our profession that we have taken the nursing hierarchy as our model. Responsibility is so diffused within this model that no one is able to take responsibility for their actions, and the only thing that travels easily up but more often down the hierarchy is blame. Professionals do not usually work within hierarchies. The professional usually has someone more experienced to whom they can turn for help and guidance, but because they take responsibility for their own actions the professional grows professionally and with responsibility. Within our hierarchy our profession is being crippled. Our responsibility is being taken away, not by anybody but just by the way we have chosen to work. This is why independent midwifery is so important to our profession.

Regional Nursing
Officer

District Nursing
Officer

Director of
Midwifery Services

Assistant Director of
Midwifery Services

Nursing Officer

Midwifery Sister

Staff Midwife

Patient

Blame travelling down
the hierarchy

With the introduction of the legislation relating to the management of the NHS under the philosophies of Roy Griffiths, the supervisor of midwives may well be the saviour of our profession within the national health service, because the role of the supervisor of midwives is enshrined in the law and at this time midwives *have* to have a supervisor.

SUPERVISION AND ANALGESIA

Pethidine and its use can be a vexed question. The woman's GP may prescribe one dose of 150 mg or the supervisor may allocate one ampoule to the independent midwife on a drug order form. Most independent midwives, however, are of the opinion that if the woman in labour is finding the pain so intolerable that she needs pethidine, she probably should not be at home and might be better being transferred to hospital where the baby can be resuscitated following the effects of the pethidine. In the home, the pain of labour is more tolerable — and often lying in a warm or hot bath can be just as effective as pethidine. Entonox apparatus can often be borrowed from the supervisor or another independent midwife, or it can be purchased from Ohmeda B.O.C. (address and prices can be found in Appendix 4).

JURISDICTION OF THE SUPERVISOR

The supervisor of midwives, when acting as supervisor and not acting in any other position of authority which she may have by reason of her position in the hierarchy of a health authority, has limited jurisdiction which involves 'general supervision' over all midwives practising within the area of the supervising authority. She ensures that midwives attend statutory or other refresher courses, and she reports to the local supervising authority any *prima facie* case of misconduct on the part of a midwife (this is when the facts show that, without some convincing explanation from the person who has been accused, an offence may have been committed).

The strongest penalty the supervisor can impose is to suspend a midwife from practice. The reasons for suspending a midwife from practice are, however, strictly controlled.

A midwife must be suspended from practice when necessary for the purpose of preventing the spread of infection. The local supervising authority may (note that the Rules say *may* and not *must*) suspend from practice until the case has been decided —

(a)   a midwife against whom it has taken proceedings before a Court of Justice.

(b)   a midwife against whom it has reported a case for investigation to a Board.

(c)   a midwife who has been referred to the Professional Conduct Committee of the Council.

(d)   a midwife who has been referred to the Health Committee of the Council.

The fact that Rule 63(2) says *may* should be carefully noted. The supervisor is therefore under a duty to examine the facts carefully and decide whether suspension is justified, particularly in the light of the fact that the Council's power is only to strike off or defer its decision if it does not dismiss the case. This is a limited power which would suggest that the intention is that only serious cases should be put to the Board's Investigating Committee. Automatic suspension without consideration of the facts is not justified nor (if from practice) in accordance with the Act of Parliament. Every supervisor has to consider carefully whether the case is one for referral to the Investigating Committee of the Board (bearing in mind its limited and very severe powers) or the hospital disciplinary machinery or whether it would be more appropriate to have a serious talk with the midwife.

So if a supervisor is just aggravated by a midwife or if they have a disagreement in philosophies, the supervisor has no jurisdiction as supervisor to impose any penalty on that midwife, unless the actions of the midwife have been such that no professional person could have acted in that way. If the supervisor sends allegations against that midwife in writing to the board, those allegations have to be placed before the Investigating Committee. Occasionally the Board receives reports which are 'for information only'. These are not retained and the Board has suggested that they should not be sent. If a supervisor has any queries, she can always telephone the Board and receive telephone advice. No action is ever taken as a result of telephone enquiries.

If a midwife is referred to the Investigating Committee of the Board, she must be sent a letter telling her what the allegations against her are and asking her for a statement or explanation. If a midwife has not received a letter, it means that she has not been reported to the Investigating Committee (unless she has recently moved house and the letter has not reached her).

The Association of Radical Midwives in its 1985 Proposals for the Future of the Maternity Service suggests that supervisors of midwives should be elected for a period of three years at a time by the midwives who are to be supervised. The premise is that these midwives would know the sort of midwife they were electing and that it would be someone who commanded respect from all the midwives who elected her — a really wise old midwife, like the emblem of the Association of Radical Midwives which is a wise old owl.

Probably the best way to help a supervisor to be a wise old owl is to treat her as such. If a midwife who works in hospital is concerned about any aspect of the care given within her unit, she can approach the supervisor of midwives with that concern. If she makes sure that she points out at the outset that she has come to see her in her role as supervisor of midwives, the whole concern can be dealt with on a purely professional level.

She can do the same when she is concerned at the way midwives are expected to practise in her unit. With all such concerns it is always better to get together one or two other midwives who will come with her to see the supervisor. This counsel of perfection, however, is almost impossible. We are often too threatened as a profession and too enfeebled and intimidated by our hierarchical structure to be able to support each other easily, and a midwife may often find herself doing this on her own. Please reread Chapter One and get yourself a support group when trying to make childbirth better for women and midwifery better for midwives.

STAFF SHORTAGES

If it is almost impossible for a midwife to provide good care to women because of shortage of staff, she has to do something about it. As a professional she is responsible for the care she gives in the unit. She is responsible for the care that is given to women, even when she is not there. She must play her part in ensuring that the care given is good.

First, she must always point out to her immediate manager if she considers that the staffing is inadequate. She must also make sure that this is recorded permanently *in writing*. This can be written on the day report or the night report. She can log it in her own diary. She should also write a letter confirming that she has pointed out the lack of staff to the immediate manager.

The midwife should also encourage others to point out staff shortages to the immediate manager and then up the hierarchy.

The Royal College of Midwives in a paper published in 1985 (RCM/139/85) gives advice to midwives working where the staffing levels are inadequate. It suggests that the midwives should find out the staffing establishment over the past two years, and that they should also look at the patient numbers over the past two years. Then they should compare their findings.

They should look at the establishment of support staff — auxiliaries, staff nurses, nursery nurses — and see whether these grades have been increased at the expense of midwives because they are cheaper.

Paragraph 8 in the Midwives' Code of Practice says — 'A midwife must not arrange for any other person than a midwife or registered medical practitioner to act as her substitute'.

The Royal College of Midwives also suggests looking at the community establishment over the past two years and at the the numbers of women cared for in the community over that period. Were more women going home earlier? Were more community clinics taking place? Were more bookings being done at home?

It should also be noted which non-midwifery duties are being done by midwives and, conversely, which midwifery duties are being carried out by people other than midwives.

The word 'midwife' means 'with woman'. It is essential that midwives care about the environment in which women have babies and about the women they serve. Midwives are not there to protect the doctors, the health authority or their managers. They are there to protect women. The duty of any professional is —

- First, to the client.
- Second, to the profession.
- Third, to the employer.

The United Kingdom Central Council for Nursing, Midwifery and Health Visiting recognises this in paragraphs 10 and 11 of its Code of Professional Conduct.

'Each registered nurse, midwife and health visitor is accountable for his or her practice, and in the exercise of professional accountability shall:

10 — Have regard to the environment of care and its physical, psychological and social effects on patients/clients, and also to the adequacy of resources, and make known to appropriate persons or authorities any circumstances which could place patients/clients in jeopardy or which militate against safe standards of practice.

11 — Have regard to the workload of and the pressures on professional colleagues and subordinates and take professional action if these are seen to be such as to constitute abuse of the individual practitioner and/or to jeopardise safe standards of practice.'

It is the duty of the midwife to inform her immediate manager of staff shortages or unsafe practices. If she gets no response she then needs to go higher in the midwifery hierarchy — to district, finally to region. She can involve the Community Health Council — which is also there for the woman. The Association for Improvements in the Maternity Services can be extremely helpful, as can the local National Childbirth Trust branch or any local birth group. The midwife can also threaten to report her managers to the Investigating Committee at the National Board, citing paragraphs 10 and 11 of the Professional Code of Conduct. In the end she may have to do that, but hopefully by then she will have improved the situation so much that this step is unnecessary.

GRIEVANCES

This quaint word is the one used when an employee feels aggrieved at how she is being treated or when a group of employees feel aggrieved at how they are being treated.

All modern employment legislation is geared to the concept of the fair and just treatment of the employee by the employer. This does not only deal with dismissal, but with all aspects of your working life.

- It is not fair or just for an employer to shout at an employee and vice versa.

- It is not fair or just for an employer to criticise an employee publicly and in front of patients or clients and vice versa.

- It is not fair or just for an employer to expect a professional person not to use her professional judgement but to obey blindly. Conversely, a professional employee should expect to use her professional skill and expertise and should not expect to obey blindly to the detriment of her professional standing and probably her client too.

- It is not fair or just for an employer to think that the employee's time belongs totally to the employer so that off duty can be changed at a moment's notice, except in a dire emergency. Conversely, the employee should expect always to come to work at the appointed time except in a dire emergency such as illness, accident or bereavement.

- It is not fair or just for an employer to make decisions about changes in working practice without consulting his or her employees. Conversely employees should consult their employer when they are deciding to change the way they work. Every contract of employment has implied in it that there is between employer and employee an obligation of mutual trust and confidence, an agreement which both sides should take seriously.

If an employee feels that she is being treated unfairly or unjustly, she can take out a grievance. She does this by writing down what she is aggrieved about. As with all such actions, it is better if this can be done as a group. But if this is not possible, it can be done as an individual.

Instances of unfair treatment need to be instanced. It is no good saying 'My senior midwife is always shouting at me'. It has to be detailed. Perhaps we should all keep a work diary. This can be just an exercise book kept in your locker into which at the end of every day you jot down what significant things happened during the day. These jottings can be totally insignificant.

Tuesday 10th May — Did a late shift (postnatal ward). On duty with Student MW Anderson — helpful and intelligent. Ten mothers and babies — quiet evening.

Or they can be very full and dynamic.

Wednesday 11th May — Early shift (postnatal ward), on duty with Student MW Anderson and S/M Freeling, twelve mothers and ten babies. Mrs Roberts fourth day caesarean section very depressed and weepy about her section. Feels the baby isn't hers, that we went and got 'any old baby' for her while she was asleep. Referred her for psychiatric opinion and discussed this with Mrs Smith (senior midwife) who said that all the women become neurotic when I am on duty.

The written grievance should be given to the manager immediately above the midwife in the hierarchy. If the grievance is against that person, this may be too difficult to do and the grievance should then be taken up to the next tier. Alternatively, the grievance can be given to the person concerned, with a copy given also to the manager above. A grievance should instance specific actions or occasions and should not just be general. The following is a well-documented and specific grievance.

We the undersigned, being midwives employed at _____, in _____ Health District wish to raise as a grievance certain complaints which we have against our senior midwife, Mrs R. Smith who is the senior midwife with responsibility for the ante and postnatal wards in this maternity unit.

We would like to point out that we are all of us registered midwives and most of us are also registered general nurses with a considerable number of years' experience, and it is our understanding of our duties that we are competent to perform them with some supervision from our senior midwife but not with the sort of detailed supervision which Mrs Smith insists on exercising over us. We also feel that Mrs Smith's treatment of us is rude and not that which one would expect from a professional colleague. The particular points of complaint are as follows.

On 12th April S/M Jones, who was the midwife in charge on Chamberlain Ward, had put a newly-delivered mother whose baby was going for adoption into Room 14 which is a single room. Mrs Smith came onto the ward while S/M Jones was at her lunch break and moved the mother in question to one of the beds in Room 12 which is a four-bedded ward, saying loudly to the student midwife while she moved her — 'That Staff Midwife Jones has no sense. We need the single rooms for women having caesareans'. S/M Jones had specifically put the mother into a single room because she anticipated that she would suffer great emotional anguish and thus needed extra privacy. Furthermore Mrs Smith should not have criticised S/M Jones in front of either a patient or student midwife.

On 14th April Mrs Smith telephoned Sister Reynolds and called her 'a stupid, careless woman'. Mrs Smith had changed the off duty, and Sister Reynolds, who had originally been on a day off, had been changed to an early shift without her knowledge. When Sister Reynolds had said that she couldn't come into work because she had made other arrangements, Mrs Smith abused her with the words above and threatened her with disciplinary action for not coming to work.

On 21st April S/M Jones took a mother she had delivered an hour previously to the bath. She had had a normal delivery, all her observations were normal and she had expressed a wish to have a bath in the bath rather than the usual blanket-bath. Mrs Smith appeared in the labour ward and criticised S/M Jones for her practice. She threatened to report S/M Jones to the Director of Midwifery Services, and she told the mother that S/M Jones was 'irresponsible'.

We would like the opportunity to discuss all these matters as a grievance in accordance with the grievance procedure.

Signed

S/M M. Jones   Sister C. Reynolds

Invoking the grievance procedure is a fairly weak and ineffectual way of having grievances sorted out because usually managers will side with each other. But a letter along those lines will curtail Mrs Smith's worst excesses for a few months, even though a grievance may have to be taken out again about six months later.

Those midwives who take out grievances, who point out staff shortages and who generally try to improve the environment for both mothers and midwives will always be seen as trouble makers. They are challenging the status quo. They will often feel vulnerable and lonely. They will hate being unpopular with their superiors. They need a support group and, if they wait long enough, they will receive feedback that their work is valued. If such midwives can become stewards for the Royal College of Midwives, this can be very supportive. They are specially protected in employment legislation as union officials. They will have the excellent RCM Labour Relations Department's help and guidance in times of need. They will also be sent for training in industrial relations. They are the conscience of our profession, the backbone of us all, the grain of sand in the oyster that produces the pearl. If that is you, thank you from us all. Remember how much we need you.

References and Further Reading

ENB (1985). *Bulletin. Issue No. 2* (Autumn). London: English National Board for Nursing, Midwifery and Health Visiting.

UKCC (1983). *Handbook of Midwives' Rules.* London: United Kingdom Central Council for Nursing, Midwifery and Health Visiting.

UKCC (1983). *Notices concerning a Midwives' Code of Practice for Midwives practising in England and Wales.* London: United Kingdom Central Council for Nursing, Midwifery and Health Visiting.

Chapter Fifteen

Research

What is actually happening to the women we are looking after? What affects them? What affects their care? Is the care we are giving the most appropriate? The most needed? The most desired?

Midwives are in a unique position to find out the answers to hundreds of questions affecting women. They are also in a very fortunate position because there is a great deal of research they can do easily, cheaply and with little effort and which will have a great influence on midwifery and obstetric practice.

It is the midwives who are there — there in the labour ward, there in the antenatal clinic, there in the postnatal ward, there in the community. It is the midwives who actually see what is happening and who have a unique opportunity to reveal it to their colleagues.

Let us start with the easiest research of all. This research needs no extra equipment, no searching for notes, no literature searches and very little effort, but it could make a useful contribution towards the way women are looked after in your unit. I am talking, of course, about research questions which can be answered by looking through the birth register which is kept on every labour ward. The following are some of the questions which can be answered by the information in the birth register.

- What sort of birth outcome do women of under 18 have in your unit?
- What sort of birth outcome do women of over 35 have in your unit?
- When women in your unit have their labour started with prostaglandin pessaries, what sort of labour outcome do they have?
- Who does episiotomies in your unit?
- When women have intact perinea, who has delivered them?
- Which women in your unit are induced? Is it women from

socioeconomic classes 1 and 2 or 2, 4, and 5? Is it women who have a prolonged pregnancy? Is it for medical reasons?

- What happens to women in your unit who are induced? How much analgesia do they have. What sort of labour outcome do they have?
- On what days of the week do women in your unit have their labours induced?
- Which are the busiest days in your labour ward? Has this anything to do with the phases of the moon (i.e. full moon, new moon)?
- What is the most popular time for babies to be born in your unit? Does this tally with the greatest number of staff being on duty?
- What percentage of women have a caesarean section in your unit?
- When women have emergency caesarean sections, how has their labour usually started?
- Why do women in your unit have planned caesarean sections?
- What percentage of women in your unit have forceps deliveries? How did their labours start? What analgesia did they have? How long were their labours?
- Who delivers the most babies in your unit?
- What proportion of deliveries in your unit are conducted by midwives? Has this varied at all in the past decade?
- When women in your unit have epidurals, what labour outcome do they have? Does this vary with the anaesthetist? Or with the midwife? Or with the obstetrician on duty?
- Does labour outcome vary when specific doctors are on duty in the labour ward?
- What happens to women in your unit who have syntocinon in labour? What analgesia do they have? What labour outcomes do they have? Do they have increased postpartum blood loss? Greater numbers of retained placentae?
- What percentage of women in your unit have retained placentae? Are there any common factors that you can see from the register?
- When do you have the fewest number of deliveries in your unit? Is it at a time when there are very few staff on duty?
- What happens to Asian women in your unit? How do they deliver? What about women from other ethnic minorites? How do they deliver?

Another source of information which is always there to do research from is the notes. The following are some questions which could be answered by studying patients' notes.

- How many different care givers did women see at the antenatal clinic?
- How many times did women come to the antenatal clinic?
- What happened to women in the different socioeconomic groups? Or in different racial or cultural groups?
- What happened to women who are under 5 ft tall? What was their birth outcome?
- What happened to women who are over 5 ft 8 inches tall. What was their labour outcome?
- How soon after they had started labour did women come in to the labour ward?
- Was there any difference in labour outcome between the women who stayed at home for three hours of their labour or eight hours of their labour?
- When do most babies' heads engage? Do multigravid women have a greater incidence of the head not engaging than primigravid women? Does it make any difference to their labour outcome?
- What useful comments are made in the antenatal notes? What comments are made in the postnatal notes?

So often we don't really know what is happening to the women we are with, but it is we the midwives who can find out. It is we who can show our colleagues what the outcome of our actions is for women. Is your hospital or unit the place I should come to if I want a normal delivery? Should I avoid delivering on a Thursday? Come on, midwives. Start looking. The women you are caring for need this information.

OBSERVATIONAL RESEARCH

When a midwife is busily rushing about doing her work, she can easily miss what is actually happening. She may learn a great deal by devoting some of her spare time to just sitting, watching what is going on and keeping notes.

A midwife could come into the antenatal clinic in her outdoor clothes and just sit and watch what actually happens. A midwife could don a nightdress and be 'transferred' from the delivery suite and then lie in bed for 24 hours 'not speaking English'. She would discover several things.

- Who gives most advice on postnatal wards?
- Who gives most care on postnatal wards?
- What breastfeeding advice is given? Is it valid?
- How many bottles are given to babies of women who want to breastfeed?
- How much dextrose or water are breastfed babies given?
- How much help is given to women who are having difficulties with breastfeeding? How many minutes in the 24 hours?
- How much food do women in the postnatal wards actually receive? Is the food nutritious, adequate in quantity, and hot?
- How much help do women have with their babies? How relevant is the teaching of procedures to women? What do they think of what they are taught?
- What are the women's impressions of their care and their carers?

A midwife could take one 'bed' under her wing, e.g. bed 14. The midwife could keep a diary of the women in that bed during a certain period. She could ask each of the women specific questions. She could observe what happens to the women in bed 14. She could produce a questionnaire for the women in bed 14 to answer. She might get some very interesting insights into what was happening in the hospital and how women perceive different things. The only problem about this type of research would be that the other staff, knowing that the woman in bed 14 was reporting back to 'her midwife', might treat her differently from other women. One way of overcoming this bias would be to choose a different bed each week.

It might be useful for the midwife to spend one of her days off each month just sitting by 'her bed' and observing what is happening.

What about tailing the postnatal ward sister for the day? What does her day consist of? How much time is spent in doctors' rounds? Drug rounds? Giving reports? How much time is spent talking to the women? What does the job of postnatal ward sister entail? What about tailing the antenatal clinic clinic sister? What does her job actually involve?

What about staff midwives in the antenatal clinic? What does their job actually entail? How much midwifery do they do? What else do they do?

Sitting in the antenatal clinic, the midwife could note how long the women wait. What are they waiting for? What happens to children who have come to the clinic? How long does the consultation with the doctor or midwife take?

In the antenatal clinic, what happens to the women who can't speak English? What happens to women who are a bit 'smelly'? What happens to women who are deaf? What happens to women who are handicapped? What happens to women who are obviously poor? What happens to women who are obviously middle class and very articulate? What happens to women solicitors or barristers? Or women doctors? Is their treatment any different from that of other women?

In the labour ward, how many people come in during a woman's labour? Who are these people? Do they knock before coming in? When they knock, do they wait until they are invited in? Or do they just knock and come straight in?

What explanations are given to women? Do they understand what they have been told? Do they feel that they had a choice?

What is happening to midwives? In the labour ward are they making decisions? Or are they being told what to do? If so, who is telling them what to do?

How much physical contact do midwives have with each other? What does the physical contact consist of? How much physical contact do midwives have with the medical staff? What about the women they are caring for? How much physical contact do midwives have with women? What sort of physical contact is it? How much physical contact do they have with husbands? What does it consist of? What about physical contact with children?

These are just a few ideas for research by observation. Much research is also done through questionnaires.

QUESTIONNAIRES

Questionnaires can be difficult, because without meaning to, you can ask biased questions. Often it is easiest to have a pilot study. In this you would ask your subjects to tell you what they would like to say about certain aspects of their care or caring, and then you would base your own questions on what they have said. Sometimes the most useful questionnaires are those with the fewest questions, for example.

St Nib's Hospital

I stayed in the hospital for _____ days after my baby was born.
What I Liked about St Nib's was _____ (then lots of space for many answers).
What I didn't like about St Nib's was _____ (then lots more space)

The disadvantage of this questionnaire is that it will only be filled in by more articulate women. This is not necessarily a disadvantage, however, because articulate women often voice the thoughts of their less articulate sisters.

The same questions can be put by community midwives, who can then feed back to the hospital very useful information about the service the hospital is providing.

In the antenatal clinic, questionnaires can be given out to women to ascertain how long they think they have waited, who they think they have been seen by, why they have come, whether they got what they came for, whether they feel encouraged to ask questions in the antenatal clinic, whether their questions were answered in a satisfactory way, how they feel about their antenatal care.

It can be useful to give a list of adjectives to people who come to the antenatal clinic asking them to circle the words which describe how they feel at that moment. Give them the same list when they leave and see what different adjectives they circle.

Please draw a circle around the words which describe how you feel at this moment.

Excited Thrilled Eager Fed-up Near to tears Happy
Enormous Bored Heavy Cold Too hot Tense Comfortable
Frustrated Angry Satisfied Stiff Depressed Frightened
Relieved Sad Impressed Loved Abandoned Well looked after
Beautiful Ugly Plain Irrelevant Important Insignificant Sexy
Gorgeous Feminine Confident Secure Intelligent Dim
Unintelligent Enthusiastic Contented Adorable Uncomfortable

The same words can be given to student midwives during different periods of their training. You can add words to test their confidence in their abilities and knowledge such as —

Confident   Clever   Knowledgeable   Significant   Useful

The changing feelings of student midwives as they go through their training will show up. The parts of the training which sap their confidence and enthusiasm might also show up.

Midwives and student midwives can be given the 'word pictures' to assess their job satisfaction.

Please draw a circle around the words which you feel describe the midwife and her job. A midwife is —

Useful   Knowledgeable   Overruled   Useless   Thick

Lacking in confidence   Influential   Valid   A minion

Clever   Bossed about   Indecisive   Important   Decisive

In charge   Unintelligent   Confident   Depressed

Unimportant   Intelligent

It would be interesting to find out which situations harm a midwife's confidence, enabling us to do something positive to stop this happening. These 'word pictures' can be anonymous and are fun to fill in and they can be useful instruments.

It is interesting to ask student midwives what their outside-of-work interests are. It is equally interesting to ask qualified midwives what their interests are. It is flattering to be asked about yourself and it is interesting for us to gain an overall impression of the people we work with.

Most units are very poor at giving women an opportunity to evaluate the care they have been given. A what-I-liked-about-my-labour-and-what-I-didn't-like evaluation would be enormously helpful if it were given to the woman soon after, or the day after, her labour. It would also be interesting if she were given the same evaluation sheet a few weeks afterwards to see if any of her priorities had changed.

Another use of questionnaires is to estimate the morbidity of or how harmful the experience of birth has been for women. Two or three months after the birth of their baby, ask women how they feel about themselves now. Have they changed a great deal since the birth of their baby? If so, how? Have they been able to make love yet? If yes, was it uncomfortable? Very sore? Fine?

In the labour ward, midwives can fill in questionnaires about how a couple or a woman react to their baby — whether they have eye-to-eye contact, whether the mother smiles, looks radiant, looks exhausted, touches her baby, talks to her baby, what adjectives she uses to describe her baby, and so on. The same sort of questionnaire could be filled in by community midwives at ten days.

Eventually we shall find a way of evaluating how satisfied a woman is with her care during labour, and we shall be able to do it in the same quick way we now do an Apgar score. After that, we shall find a way of evaluating how content and useful we have helped her partner to feel.

We could also use a questionnaire to find out what makes it difficult for midwives to give the sort of care they want to give to women, and what midwives think their training has done to them and what it has given them. The questions we need to answer are limitless.

RANDOMISED CONTROL TRIALS

One of the most effective ways of answering a question is to compare two matched groups. This way you can see what effect a certain treatment has on a group compared to the group which does not have that treatment. Probably the easiest and most effective way of doing this is by randomising. Before randomising, you need a list of criteria into which the women must fit. For example —

The women must be over 5 ft in height, primigravidae, with a single fetus presenting by the vertex, in spontaneous labour.

or

The women must be para one or two, under 38 years, in spontaneous labour with a single fetus presenting by the vertex.

Having decided on your criteria, you need to decide on the number of women you are going to compare. The simpler the research, the easier it is to finish. The smaller the numbers, the easier it is to analyse.

Forty women would probably be plenty for a pilot research project. Then you decide on what you are going to ask each group. For instance, Jenny Sleep, when looking at the carrying out of episiotomies by midwives, gave two different instructions to midwives, either —

Avoid an episiotomy.

or

Avoid a tear.

For the midwife looking at the use of syntometrine, the instructions could be —

Give syntometrine with the birth of the anterior shoulder.

Do not give syntometrine.

Give syntometrine after the cord has stopped pulsating.

These instructions could be in an envelope with relevant questions to be answered by the midwife conducting the third stage.

There needs to be an equal number of women in each group. So for someone doing the above syntometrine trial, the number would need to be divisible by three, such as 42 women in three groups of 14.

Some of the myths of midwifery could be looked at too.

Does a squirt of breast milk in a baby's sticky eye cure the infection?

What about cord care? What about a randomised control trial comparing the use of spirit, water and nothing to help a baby's cord separate?

If the differing instructions are put into sealed envelopes which are then jumbled up and placed in a pile, the care giver will not know what instructions will be in the envelope.

With our Know Your Midwife scheme, we first make sure that the women fall into the following criteria:

- Over 5 ft in height.
- No previous uterine surgery.
- No more than two TOPs or miscarriages.

- No previous intra-uterine growth retardation.
- No previous stillbirths or neonatal deaths.
- No gross medical conditions.

When we have a pile of notes fitting in with this description, we then pin envelopes on each set of notes. Inside the envelope is a piece of paper and on it is written either Know Your Midwife Scheme or Control Group. Half the envelopes contain one message and half contain the other. You cannot tell which is which from the outside of the envelope.

In this way we should end up with two equal sized groups of women. If the randomisation has been done properly, all other factors should be equal, such as socioeconomic class, smokers and non-smokers, drinkers and non-drinkers, primigravid women and multigravid women, English and non-English speaking women and so on.

OTHER POINTS TO REMEMBER WHEN DOING RESEARCH

If the women are to be approached or affected in any way, their permission has to be asked for before they are included in the research.

For any research (other than that carried out by going through the birth register or notes), a proposal must be put before an Ethical Committee if there is one in your hospital or health authority. Obviously for any observational research or before giving out questionnaires, the senior midwife running the unit needs to be asked for her permission. For any research which changes the treatment of women (such as investigating the use of syntometrine), the obstetricians need to be asked for their permission. For any research which changes the treatment of babies (such as investigating cord care or eye care), the paediatricians need to be asked for their permission.

If you want to look at a particular question, it is important to see whether other people have asked the same question and what they have discovered. This involves a search of the relevant medical and nursing literature.

If you have access to a good library, you are blessed indeed. The libraries attached to teaching hospitals can be excellent. The librarian at the Royal College of Midwives is enormously helpful, as are the librarians at the Royal College of Nursing library. There is an excellent library at the King's Fund Centre. Librarians are the stepping stone to much research. Do not be shy to ask them anything you need to know. They have an enormous amount of knowledge at their fingertips, and they can save you hours of searching. Often they will do a computer search for you for the relevant literature in just a couple of days.

FINANCIAL HELP

Simple research projects will take time but will not involve a financial outlay except for the odd exercise book and pen. But some research projects start off and become larger. This will have financial implications — the project may require you to employ help, print questionnaires, post material or take time off to pursue it further. For midwives there are several sources of funds, and many of them do not have enough applicants from our profession. A list of bodies offering research grants is in Appendix 2.

Before applying for a research grant, be aware of the emotional implications of money. Money causes great jealousy, and you may find that you are getting much more than just money when you are awarded a grant. Having said that, remember that the future care of women and their babies depends on you. If you can keep that vision in front of you, you will be able to cope with any envy or jealousy the award of money brings you.

A research proposal can be set out as follows —

Name   *Qualifications*

Place of work

Address

Title of project (One sentence)

Abstract of research (The project in a nutshell — about 200 words describing the project.)

Duration of project (How long you anticipate it will take to do.)

Financial support required (This needs to be detailed.)

Supervision (The name of a researcher of standing within your unit who will make sure your research is conducted properly, or the names of the people in your steering group. It is helpful to have some of the members of your steering group come from outside your own unit so that they have an all-round view. Many midwives have been very grateful for the advice and support so generously given to researchers by the National Perinatal Epidemiology Unit at the John Radcliffe Infirmary, Oxford.)

Details of the proposed investigation
(Start with the background to the study, i.e. why you think it needs to be investigated. Then go on to detail why you are doing the study — the purpose of it. Then detail how you will be doing the study. Say what data and what information you will be collecting.)
References (List books and papers which are relevant.)
Curriculum vitae of applicant(A resumé of who you are, what qualifications you have and any other information that you think may be relevant or interesting.)

The research proposal I have shown is a very detailed one and you may want to adapt it to fit your needs, but you will still need to include most of the information listed above. Good luck with your project. Remember to write about it at the end and to send the report to one of the nursing or midwifery journals. If it improves the way women are looked after, if you achieve nothing else in your life, you will have done a wonderful thing. Your study will influence the way our granddaughters give birth and will ensure a midwifery profession that is stronger than it was before you did your research — thank you from us all.

References and Further Reading

Grant, A. (1982). Evaluating midwifery practice: the role of the randomised controlled trial. *Research and the Midwife Conference Proceedings 1982*. Available from Nursing Education Research Unit, King's College, London University.

Sleep, J. (1984). Episiotomy in normal delivery — management of the perineum. *Nursing Times*; 80(47): 28–30 (November 21), and *Nursing Times*; 80(48): 51–4 (November 28).

Sleep, J., Grant, A., Garcia, J., Elbourne, D., Spencer, J., Chalmers, I. (1984). West Berkshire perineal management trial. *British Medical Journal*; 289: 587–90 (September 8).

Chapter Sixteen

The Next Steps

Throughout this book I have emphasised how important it is to set up a support group that can love and cherish you. Only in this way can midwives be strong enough to take on the enormous task ahead of them. Only in this way can they be strong enough to support and cherish each other.

I suggest that having other people to support and cherish you is the most important factor for the future of our profession. When those 'supporters' are mothers who you have looked after during childbirth, it will give you much much more than the emotional support that you greatly need. It will also give you access to families with babies and access to what women are saying and how they are feeling. It means that you become a midwife (someone who is 'with woman') rather than seeing the woman as 'other' or different. Your intimate knowledge of women will strengthen you and help you to protect them from practices which are harmful to them.

Having got your support group organised (your support group can begin with just one other person, don't forget), you will begin to feel stronger, more cherished and more aware of the fundamental strands running through our profession and its involvement with women. It is time to look about you and set about your personal growth as a midwife, to decide what you can do to take our profession forward.

How do you practise midwifery? Are you totally supportive of women? Do you help them to have a choice, to take up a position they would prefer, to give birth where and how they would like?

How are you able to work within your own unit? Can you truly practise as a professional midwife — taking decisions which are within your competence, feeling confident and supported, respected for your knowledge, your opinions listened to, your thoughts respected?

Do not tell me that you are 'only a staff midwife' or 'only a senior midwife' or 'only' anything else. This is the reason that the hierarchical structure of midwifery is so damaging to us (which may well have been why it was set up in the first place). When you work within a hierarchy, there is always someone over you, there is always someone above you who can criticise or blame you. That is why it cripples us so much. One of our aims as a profession has to be to work out a better structure for ourselves. We must all think about this problem and eventually a solution will emerge and evolve. It already is emerging a bit at the moment with both the Association of Radical Midwives and the Royal College of Midwives discussing how to achieve more community-based care. It has been suggested that midwives could work in teams or group practices, mainly in the community, carrying out more domino deliveries and home deliveries. Referral would be direct to a midwife in early pregnancy, with that midwife having access to hospital maternity beds and able to make direct referrals to a consultant obstetrician.

You probably work within the hierarchy at this moment, and you are well aware that above you and among your peers are many many midwives who are more 'experienced' than you are. This concept of 'experience' is often a red herring and is really another name for length of service. Obviously there are and always will be other midwives who really are 'more experienced' than you are, but if the word 'experienced' is being used as a substitute for 'marking time' it is meaningless.

Experiences can be lived through, existed through, or can be times of enormous growth and learning, with you being aware of many things going on, much happening around you, and the deeper meaning behind much of what is happening.

One of the easiest ways to learn a great deal as you work is to make sure that you see a woman or some women all the way through their pregnancies, labours and the puerperium. When you are really 'with women', by their side, at their right hand throughout this huge life-changing experience, you will gain enormous knowledge and experience. The fragmented care we give most women at the moment might almost have been designed to stop us from learning about our role and to weaken us as a profession.

When you are working in an area where you are unable to relate to a woman or to women, because you have never met them before or because they are in a state of such stress that they are unable to relate to you (as in the labour ward) or because there are too many of them to relate to (as in most antenatal clinics and postnatal wards), you are being prevented from forming a deep relationship with the women in your care. Yet this is her greatest need — to relate closely to someone during her pregnancy, labour and puerperium. She needs to do this so that she can trust that person enough to be able to surrender to the whole experience when she is in labour and, afterwards, so that she can come to terms with motherhood.

She is not alone with this deep need to form a loving and supportive relationship with you. You also have this deep need. You probably became a midwife because you feel close to women and care about what happens to them, and obviously you care about what happens to you.

You are probably someone who can be very loving and cherishing to other people, as well as someone who needs to be loved and cherished by other people. This is an entirely normal human need and, when we split up the relationship between two individuals, we leave them both feeling bereft and full of grief. Because we have created such an abnormal situation (a woman going through the most intimate and stressful experience of her life surrounded by strangers), we are all prone to feel terribly uncomfortable and full of grief and anger.

We cope with these terribly strong emotions by denying them, by pretending that the way we work is 'normal', that midwives must not get over-involved with their 'patients', that the women are 'other' — separate beings, with nothing in common with people like you and me. But our reason tells us that this woman is my sister, my best friend, myself. Sometimes the conflict this deeper knowledge brings is just too painful to bear, and we are unable to suppress our feelings. We either have to get out (into health visiting, teaching, administration, anything) or we pretend almost successfully to ourselves and to others that these women are not really my sister, my best friend, myself, that these women really *are* 'other' and have nothing in common with me. With this huge and painful denial, we cripple ourselves emotionally and limit our effectiveness and growth, but at least we suffer no more pain.

This is why at the beginning of this book I pointed out that our profession is at the moment emotionally impoverished. We have created and we have to work within a system which is unable to cope with the human and emotional needs of its members. Isobel Menzies in her brilliant and (sadly) timeless article. 'The Functioning of social systems as a defence against anxiety', describes the social systems of nursing. She notes that depersonalisation, the denial of significance of the individual, the denial of feelings, and the tendency to reduce the weight of responsibility in decision-making by checks and counter-checks are very common in nursing. They are also common in midwifery.

How can we help ourselves and the women we are with to overcome this enormous and seemingly intractable handicap, without leaving the profession (as four out of every five midwives do) and without becoming too damaged in the process?

Our strength is within us — we have the knowledge. After all, during training each student midwife should —

(a) personally make antenatal examination of at least 100 pregnant women, including giving the appropriate advice;
(b) give supervision and care to at least 40 pregnant women;
(c) receive clinical instruction in the conduct of labour, including the witnessing of ten normal labours;
(d) personally manage the labour and conduct the delivery of not less than 40 women, under the supervision of midwives;
(e) receive instruction on the indications for, and the technique of, episiotomy, including the safe strength and dosage of local anaesthetics, followed by practical experience;
(f) receive instruction on the technique of repairing the perineum and practical experience, as appropriate;
(g) attend/assist at not less than 40 complicated labours;
(h) attend at least one or two breech deliveries;
(i) personally examine 100 mothers during the postnatal period;
(j) personally examine 100 newborn babies;
(k) have experience in supervision and care of mothers and babies, including low birth weight, post-term and ill newborn babies.

We have the skills to enable normal birth to take place. We have the affection and caring of the women we have been with during childbirth. In terms of economics, we are vastly superior to other types and approaches to care. The midwife's care is very cheap. This not just because she is paid too little (although she is). It is because she relies on the human body and not on technological instruments which cost a lot of money. (Hence the involvement of big business in maternity care — those working lunches are not given because the manufacturers are philanthropic organisations which want to make sure that doctors are well nourished. Businesses want to make huge amounts of money for their shareholders, and childbirth is big business — as long as it can be made abnormal.) The midwife with her Pinard's stethoscope who uses one or two pairs of sterilised gloves during the whole process is a very cheap option. The fact that she is often also a very safe option is purposely overlooked. She makes no money for anyone. This factor, at a time of economic stringency, will emerge and will help the midwife to develop professionally.

Once we have set up support systems for ourselves outside our profession, with the women who love us and whom we love, it is time for us to set up support systems within our workplace. A support system consists of a small number of people who know, trust and care about each other. They need to make a commitment to meet each other regularly, at least every week. They can start by telling each other about themselves and about who they are. Physical contact is important and can be achieved in a non-threatening way. The group, or the pair, just hold hands for a few seconds, preferably with their eyes shut. There are many non-threatening 'touching' games in Martin Jelf's *Manual for Action*. Meg Bond's book, *Stress and Self-awareness: a Guide for Nurses*, contains a lot of excellent material about how to set up support groups.

For the first few weeks, the members of the support group will just need to let off steam — to grumble at the injustices and the ridiculous way everything is organised. After a few weeks, however, they will begin to think about what they want to achieve, about how they want to take their profession forward.

One good way of strengthening midwives' self-confidence is to take on responsibility for a specific group of women and to care for those women as a team, so that each midwife gets to know the women and vice versa. This can be done in two ways, depending on the self-confidence and vision of your senior managers.

1. The members of the support group go to see their head midwife and suggest the idea to her — working out with her how they can achieve it.

2. The members of the support group can start slowly with just one woman who they take under their wing and whose care they share between themselves.

Any change is very threatening to people within the sort of hierarchy that we work in. Even the action of two midwives looking after a very few women can threaten and intimidate. It is impossible to achieve change for all women all at once. We have to make things better for one, then two, then three women. If we can work as a small team — a group practice of midwives — this is immediately strengthening for us and provides an in-built support group.

Even though it is hard to achieve the care of a few women, it is very worthwhile for the strength and the learning experience it will give you. It can be arranged in just the same way as it would if a colleague who was your best friend came in to have a baby.

Jane books at the hospital. She is booked by her friend Dora. Dora accompanies Jane to her examination by the doctor and books Jane for her next antenatal appointment. At that appointment Dora and Josie, another midwife, are both in the hospital. Josie actually conducts the antenatal examination but Dora pops down to see them both. This forms the basis of all Jane's antenatal care. She is always seen by Dora or Josie and, if ever she has to see a doctor, one of them goes with her.

When Jane gets to 36 weeks of pregnancy, Dora and Josie give her their home telephone numbers and details of where she can contact them week by week. They often ring her between her antenatal visits to see how she is and to show her that they care about her.

When Jane goes into labour, whichever midwife is free attends her throughout her labour and delivery. Afterwards they both help towards her care in the postnatal period. By looking after someone you know like this, you will be strengthened and made more articulate.

Jane is not getting special care. She is getting normal care. It is the other women who are receiving substandard care. What if any abnormalities develop, you might be asking? What if they do? We work with many doctors — we can always accompany her when we refer her to a doctor. Also remember, 70–80% of women are going to get through their pregnancies and labours safely and without need of any medical assistance.

Remember the phrase in the *Role of the Midwife* — 'It appears to be readily acknowledged that the midwife is responsible for the care of normal childbirth, but perhaps one of the main threats to the execution of that role is the practical application of the philosophy that childbirth is only normal in retrospect.'

The philosophy that 'childbirth is only normal in retrospect' is not only damaging to the midwife's role, it is damaging to women. It interferes with the progress of normal childbirth because it raises the anxiety levels surrounding the woman during this very impressionable time.

You also need some facts at your fingertips. The Midwives' Information and Resource Service will send you a big bundle of information in a folder, every three months (its address is in Appendix 3). This will increase your knowledge. It will also help you to counter arguments and attempts to persuade you to do things that you feel are not in the best interests of the woman. The Current Awareness Service at the Royal College of Midwives will send you references every two months and for a small charge will photocopy those articles you would like to have. When you have some facts at your fingertips, you will be strengthened and more articulate

'Why haven't you ruptured the membranes yet?'

'I'm very influenced by the work of Kay Mordecai Robson who found that a woman had a 90% chance of feeling some immediate affection for her baby if she did *not* have her membranes artificially broken. She had a 74% chance of experiencing indifference to her baby if her membranes were artificially ruptured.'

'I have always been interested in the work of Robert Caldeyroy Barcia who questioned the artificial rupturing of the membranes because of the increase in disalignment of the parietal bones and the increase of hypoxia associated with this practice.'

I find it better to literally have these facts at my fingertips. I always carry around with me a folder — the type which has lots of plastic envelopes in it. In these I carry the research reports I need to refer to most often. I feel stronger when I know that I can quote from them there and then. I can also let other people read them and so increase the amount of knowledge in the place where I work.

The other work which is essential reading for any midwife is Sally Inch's book *Birthrights*. In it she has hundreds of references. It is a mine of information.

The work of MacVicar shows that women who are having babies now are healthier and less at risk than any generation in the past (the increasing levels of unemployment may affect these statistics later on). Midwives have more access to information than at any other time in their history. They are more aware of the economy of their practice than they have ever been before. They are more aware of the love and support of women than ever before.

With women we need to develop a more sensitive way of providing care, perhaps developed along the lines of the 1986 Association of Radical Midwives' *Proposals for the Future of the Maternity Services*. They propose that —

- The parturient woman be the central person in the process of care.
- Midwives' skills be fully utilised.
- There be continuity of care for all women.
- There be choice in childbirth for women.
- There be accountability of services to the consumer.

Together we can make childbirth the joyous, growing, confidence-enhancing experience it can and should be. But the person it must start with, the person it all hinges on, the person on whom it all depends is

YOU

SENSITIVE MIDWIFE.

References and Further Reading

Arms, S. (1975). *Immaculate Deception*. Boston: The San Francisco Book Company/Houghton Mifflin Books.

Association of Radical Midwives (1986). Draft proposal for the future of the maternity services. London: ARM.

Bond, M. (1986). *Stress and Self-awareness: a Guide for Nurses*. London: Heinemann Nursing.

Caldeyro-Barcia, R. (1979). *Physiological and Psychological Bases for the Modern and Humanised Management of Normal Labour*. Scientific Publication No. 858 of the Centro Latino Americano de Perinatologia y Desarrollo Humano: Montevideo, Uraguay.

Central Midwives' Board: *Approved Midwifery Training Syllabus*.

Central Midwives' Board Scotland, Northern Ireland Council for Nurses and Midwives, An Bord Altranais, Central Midwives' Board (1983). *The Role of the Midwife*.

Inch, S. (1982). *Birthrights*. London: Hutchinson Ltd.

Jelfs, M. (1982). *Manual for Action*. London: Action Resources Group (Available from 13 Mornington Grove, London E3 4NS).

MacVicar, J. (1981). Changing birth patterns during a period of declining births. *Maternal and Child Health*; 280–4 (July).

Menzies, I. (1960). *The Functioning of Social Systems as a Defence Against Anxiety*. London: The Tavistock Institute of Human Relations.

Mordecai Robson, K. (1982). I feel nothing. *Nursing Mirror*; 154(25): 24–7 (June 23).

Appendix 1
Further Reading

Arms S. (1975). *Immaculate Deception*. San Francisco and Boston: San Francisco Book Company/Houghton Mifflin Book Co.
Beels C. (1978). *The Childbirth Book*. London: Turnstone Books.
Boyd C., Sellers L. (1982). *The British Way of Birth*. London: Pan.
Breen D. (1981). *Talking with Mothers*. R. J. Acford Ltd.
Cartwright A. (1979). *The Dignity of Labour?* London: Tavistock.
Chard T., Richards M. (1977). *Benefits and Hazards of the New Obstetrics*. London: Spastics International Medical Publications.
Cohen N. W., Estner L. J. (1983). *Silent Knife*. Bergin and Garvey.
Courter G. (1981). *The Midwife*. London: Signet Books.
Davis E. (1981). *A Guide to Midwifery Heart and Hands*. London: Bantam Books.
Delamont S. (1980). *The Sociology of Women—An Introduction*. London: George Allen & Unwin.
Evans R., Durward L. (1984). *Maternity Rights Handbook*. Harmondsworth: Penguin.
Fraser A. (1984). *The Weaker Vessel*. London: Weidenfeld & Nicolson.
Friday N. (1976). *My Secret Garden—Women's Sexual Fantasies*. London: Quartet.
Gaskin I. M. (1978). *Spiritual Midwifery*. Summertown. Available from the Book Publishing Company, The Farm, 156 Drakes Lane, Summertown, TN 38483 USA.
Greer G. (1984). *Sex and Destiny. The Politics of Human Fertility*. London: Picador.
Inch S. (1982). *Birthrights*. London: Hutchinson.
Kitzinger S. (1978). *Women as Mothers*. London: William Collins and Sons and Company Ltd.
Kitzinger S. (1979). *Birth at Home*. Oxford: Oxford University Press.
Kitzinger S. (1979). *The Experience of Breast Feeding*. Harmondsworth: Pelican.
Kitzinger S. (1980). *Pregnancy and Childbirth*. London: Michael Joseph.
Kitzinger S. (1983). *The New Good Birth Guide*. Harmondsworth: Penguin.
Kitzinger S. (1983). *Woman's Experience of Sex*. London: Dorling Kindersley.
Lang R. (1972). *The Birth Book*. London: Genesis Press.

MacFarlane A., Mugford M. (1984). *Birth Counts—Statistics of Pregnancy and Childbirth*. Norwich: HMSO. (two volumes).

McKay S. (1983). *Assertive Childbirth*. Englewood Cliffs, NJ: Prentice-Hall Inc.

Menzies I. (1970). *The Functioning of Social Systems as a Defence Against Anxiety*. London: The Tavistock Institute of Human Relations.

Messenger M. (1982). *The Breastfeeding Book*. London: Century Publishing Company Ltd.

Monaco M., Junor V. (1980). *Home Birth Handbook*. Bija Press.

Oakley A. (1979). *From Here to Maternity—Becoming a Mother*. Harmondsworth: Pelican Books Ltd.

Oakley A. (1980). *Women Confined*. Martin Robertson & Co Ltd.

Oakley A. (1981). *Subject Women*. London: Fontana.

Oakley A. (1984). *The Captured Womb*. Oxford: Blackwell.

Odent M. (1984). *Entering the World, the De-Medicalization of Childbirth*. Marion Boyers Ltd.

Odent M. (1984). *Birth Reborn*. London: Souvenir Press.

O'Driscoll K., Meagher D. (1980). *Active Management of Labour*. Philadelphia: W. B. Saunders Co Ltd.

Prince J., Adams M. E. (1978). *Minds, Mothers and Midwives, the Psychology of Childbirth*. Harlow: Longman Group Ltd.

Rich A. (1981). *Of Woman Born*. London: Virago.

Rothman B. K. (1982). *In Labour—Women and Power in the Birthplace*. London: Junction Books Ltd.

Scully D. (1980). *Men who Control Women's Health*. Boston: Houghton Mifflin Company.

Stanway A., Stanway P. (1984). *Choices in Childbirth*. London: Pan.

Stewart & Stewart, (1976). *Safe Alternatives in Childbirth*. NAPSAC.

Townsend P., Davidson N. (1982). *Inequalities in Health—The Black Report*. Harmondsworth: Pelican.

Wright E. (1964). *The New Childbirth*. Tandem Publishing Ltd.

Zander L., Chamberlain G. (1984). *Pregnancy Care for the 1980s*. London: The Royal Society of Medicine.

Appendix 2

Where to Apply for a Research Grant

MAWS MIDWIVES' RESEARCH SCHOLARSHIP

Information from the Royal College of Midwives, 15 Mansfield Street, London W1M 0BE, 01 580 6523. An award of £1000. Closing date end of May. For a midwife to research any aspect of midwifery practice, education or management within the midwifery service.

ELIZABETH CLARK CHARITABLE TRUST

Information from Miss Vera Darling, 429 Brighton Road, Croydon CR2 6UD. Awards of £250–£1000. Closing date the beginning of January. To look in depth at clinical aspects of patient care relevant to your work.

BIRTHRIGHT

Royal College of Obstetricians and Gynaecologists, 27 Sussex Place, Regent's Park, London NW1 4RG, 01 262 5425. Awards of up to £35,000. Closing date the end of January.

WELLINGTON NURSING RESEARCH BURSARY

The Wellington Foundation, Wellington Place, London NW8. Awards of up to £7000. Closing date middle of June.

DHSS GRANTS

Information from The Secretary, Small Grants Committee, Department of Health and Social Security, Alexander Fleming House, Elephant and Castle, London SE1 6BY. Awards of up to £30,000.

LOCALLY ORGANISED RESEARCH GRANTS

Contact the Secretary of the Regional Research Committee at your Regional Health Authority. She or he will tell you how to apply for one of their grants.

HOSPITAL SAVING ASSOCIATION NURSING SCHOLARSHIP

Scholarships awarded to SRNs who are pursuing further education. Application forms from The Hospital Saving Association Charitable Trust, Hambledon House, Andover, Hants SP10 1LQ. Tel: 0264 53211.

JOHNSON & JOHNSON TRAVEL AWARDS

Information from the Director of Education, The Royal College of Midwives' Trust, 15 Mansfield St, London W1M 0BE. £1000 to look at areas of midwifery in England or overseas, or to attend a major conference. Closing date end of April.

WINSTON CHURCHILL MEMORIAL TRUST

Travelling fellowships to pay for travelling and accommodation costs for 4–10 weeks. Information from 15 Queen's Gate Terrace, London SW7 5PR. Tel: 01 584 9315.

NATIONAL FLORENCE NIGHTINGALE MEMORIAL COMMITTEE of GREAT BRITAIN & NORTHERN IRELAND

Information from 6 Grosvenor Crescent, London SW1X 7EH. Tel: 01 235 0186. Travel awards for either abroad or the UK to study anything connected with nursing. Closing date end of October.

SIR JULES THORN RESEARCH SCHOLARSHIP

For a RGN, EN or midwife to study at university for two years full time for a research degree—also administered by the Florence Nightingale Memorial Committee.

COW & GATE OPEN SCHOLARSHIP FOR MIDWIVES

Information from The Director of Education, The Royal College of Midwives Trust, 15 Mansfield St, London W1M 0BE. £1000 to fund a study or project to be undertaken, or a conference to be visited or experience to be gained. Closing date end of May.

THE IOLANTHE TRUST

Information from the Administrative Secretary, Iolanthe Trust, 15 Mansfield St, London W1M 0BE. Grants for training, education and professional development and research in the field of midwifery. Closing date end of February.

MILTON EDUCATIONAL AWARDS FOR MIDWIVES

Information from the Director of Education, The Royal College of Midwives, 15 Mansfield St, W1M 0BE. £1500 for a midwife to further her education by attending a relevant course of study or a conference. Closing date end of March.

FARLEY HEALTH PRODUCTS AWARD FOR MIDWIVES

Information from Director of Education, The Royal College of Midwives' Trust, 15 Mansfield St, London W1M 0BE. £1000 for a newly (not more than two years) qualified midwife to undertake or complete a project related to clinical practice or to travel within the UK or Europe to observe midwifery practice. Closing date end of May.

ANNUAL BOUNTY COMPETITION FOR MIDWIVES

Information from Director of Education, Royal College of Midwives, 15 Mansfield St, London W1M 0BE. A presentation by a midwife of a poster, flip chart, leaflet, tape/slide presentation, video or film script, to improve communications between midwives and the families they care for. Differing subjects each year. Closing date beginning of September. £1000.

NURSING TIMES/3M NATIONAL NURSING AWARDS

Awards for nurses, midwives and health visitors for innovation in the fields of research, practice, management or education. £1000 for the winner and £1000 for the project. NT/3M National Nursing Awards, 4 Little Essex St, London WC2R 3LF. Closing date mid April.

Many of these grants are administered by the Royal College of Midwives and it is often, but not always, necessary to have been a member for two years.

Appendix 3
Libraries

THE ROYAL COLLEGE OF MIDWIVES LIBRARY

11 Queen Anne St, London W1M 0BE. Tel: 01 580 6523.
Tremendously helpful librarian, Current Awareness Service, help with
information when starting a literature search, photocopying facilities,
information retrieval.

MIDWIVES' INFORMATION & RESOURCE SERVICE

National Temperance Hospital, 112 Hampstead Road, London NW1
2LT. Tel: 01 387 3755.
No thinking midwife should be without a subscription (£15 year) to the
regular information packs which cover all aspects of midwifery
—research, news, clinical practice, management and education gleaned
from hundreds of journals, books, magazines, newspapers, research
conferences etc. Also regular fact packs on particular subjects pertinent
to midwifery and childbirth. Workshops to help midwives develop
specific skills. Networking with international midwife contacts. Future
plans include computerised literature searches.

KINGS FUND CENTRE LIBRARY

Kings Fund Centre, 126 Albert Street, London NW1 7NF. Tel: 01 267
6111.
Big reference library with every periodical and journal you can think of.
Photocopying facilities and literature searches. Comfortable and warm
to work in, librarians helpful.

ROYAL SOCIETY OF MEDICINE LIBRARY

1 Wimpole St, London W1M 8AE. Tel: 01 408 2119.
A wonderful library, photocopying facilities, literature searches,

almost any medical journal you could think of, helpful librarians, warm and comfortable place to go and read and study. To join the Maternity Forum costs £25 a year and gives the member access to use of the library for reference only as well as entrance to a series of fascinating multidisciplinary meetings on maternity care. To become a full member costs £95 a year and enables member to borrow books.

WOMEN'S RESEARCH AND RESOURCES CENTRE

The Hungerford House, Embankment Place, London WC2N 6PA. Tel: 01 930 0715.

YOUR LOCAL POSTGRADUATE MEDICAL LIBRARY

Go and see the librarian. If you are doing some studying, either a recognised course or a piece of study for yourself, they are usually most helpful and accommodating. In some hospitals the midwives can use the medical library at all times. If you can't in your hospital, go and talk with the librarian. Books are for reading. Journals are for learning from. Librarians are a special breed of people who love books and want to share that love with everyone they come into contact with.

Appendix 4

Equipment and Stockists

ENTONOX

Equipment in carrying bag from Medishield, Harlow, Elizabeth Way, Harlow, Essex CM19 5AB. Tel: 0279 442001.
Costs (1986) £287.75p plus £43.16p VAT—Total £330.91p.

Cylinders of Entonox

B.O.C., P.O. Box 17, Medical Works, Gt West Road, Brentford, Middx TW8 9AL. Tel: 01 560 3123.
Size D 500 L £2.79p per cylinder plus 90p per cylinder per month rental.

HAEMOGLOBIN METER

Timesco of London, 176 Pentonville Road, London N1 9JP. Tel: 01 278 0712/3.

VARIED EQUIPMENT

Porter Nash Medical, 116 Wigmore Street, London W1H 9FD. Tel: 01 486 1434.

FOR VERY REASONABLY PRICED EQUIPMENT

Pulse—Doctors' Shop, Morgan Grampian House, 30 Calderwood St, Woolwich, London SE18 6QH. Tel: 01 855 7777 Ext 454 or 574.
Nurses' stethoscope £4.50.
7 inch Mayo needleholders £4.50
7 inch Spencer Wells forceps (2 needed) £3.95
6 inch dissecting forceps £1.75
7 inch Mayo scissors £3.25

A portable sphygmomanometer can be brought for £14.50 Model HT-100 from Tohto Tsusho (UK) Ltd, PO Box 366, Magdelen House, High Roding, Dunmow, Essex. Tel: Great Dunmow (0371) 3082

EQUIPMENT CAN ALSO BE OBTAINED FROM

Pan Servico Ltd, 436 Streatham High Road, London SW16 1DA. Tel: 01 764 1806 or 01 679 2489.
John Bell & Croyden, (Savory & Moore Ltd.) 54 Wigmore St, London W1H 0AU. Tel: 01 935 5555.
Arterial Medical Services Ltd., Arterial House, 313 Chase Road, Southgate, London N14 6JH. Tel: 01 882 4434.
Surgikos Ltd., Kirkton Campus, Livingston, West Lothian, EH54 7AT. Tel: 0506 413441.
For sterile gloves.
Delivery packs (£5.50p each) which contain cord clamp, baby wrap, sterile sheets, trays for lotions and sterile dressings.
Robinsons of Chesterfield, Robinson and Son, Surgical Dressings, Wheat Bridge, Chesterfield, Derby. Tel: 0246 31101.

YOUR LOCAL CHEMIST FOR

Inco pads, heating pads for babies, mucous extractors, thermometers etc.
For syntometrine and ergometrine quote Schedule 4 Part 3 of the Medicines (Prescription Only) Order 1980 and the Medicines Act 1968 (Part 3).

BLEEPERS

British Telecom, 81 Newgate Street, London EC1A 7AJ. Tel: Dial 100 and ask for Freephone Radiopaging. Many other radiopaging services in the Yellow Pages.

CAR PHONES

See Yellow Pages or local adverts.

BLOOD TESTS

Most NHS Hospitals with haematology departments will test blood for you and will invoice you. Otherwise ring your local private hospital and ask what private haematology services they use.

Metpath, 134 Harley St, London W1. Tel: 01 486 0669.
Shanks Laboratories, 81 Harley St, London W1. Tel: 01 935 7710.

BABY SCALES

Portable baby scales can most easily be found in angling shops which have a large variety of portable scales, but kitchen scales with a large bowl can be used when the baby is small.

REGISTERS

These are available from Hymns Ancient and Modern: Register II costs £1.95, including VAT, postage and packing. The address is St Mary's Works, St Mary's Plain, Norwich, Norfolk NR3 3BH.

Appendix 5

Addresses of Organisations You May Need to Use

Spaces have been left for local contacts that are useful to know of before the event.

Active Birth Movement, 18 Laurier Road, London NW5 1SG. Tel: 01 267 3006.

Association of Radical Midwives, 8A The Drive, Wimbledon, London SW20.

My local contact is _____

Association for Improvements in the Maternity Services, Hon. Subscriptions Secretary, Elizabeth Key, Goose Green Barn, Moss House Lane, Much Hoole, Preston, Lancs. PR4 4TD.

Excellent newsletter. I last renewed my subscription (£6) on _____

Association for Postnatal Illness, Queen Charlotte's Hospital, Goldhawk Road, London W6. Tel: 01 741 5019 or 7 Gowan Avenue, Fulham, SW6.

My local contact is _____

Alcoholics Anonymous, 11 Redcliffe Gardens, London SW10. Tel: 01 352 9779.

Association of Breastfeeding Mothers, 131 Mayow Road, London SE26. Tel: 01 778 4769.

My local contact is _____

Association to Combat Huntington's Chorea, Borough House, 34A Station Road, Hinckley, Leics LE10 1AP. Tel: 0455 615558.

Association for Spina Bifida and Hydrocephalus, 22 Upper Woburn Place, London WC1H 0EP. Tel: 01 388 1382.

My local contact is _____

British Diabetic Association, 10 Queen Anne St, London W1M 0BD. Tel: 01 323 1531.

My local contact is _____

British Epilepsy Association, Crowthorne House, New Wokingham Road, Wokingham, Berks RG11 3AY. Tel: 0344 773122.

British Pregnancy Advisory Service, Austy Manor, Wootton Wawen, Solihull, West Midlands, B95 6DA. Tel: 05642 3225.

Brook Advisory Centres, Central Office, 153A East St, London SE17 2SD. Tel: 01 708 1234.

Caesarean Support Network, 11 Duke St, Astley, Lancs, M29 7BG. Tel: 0942 878076. Or 52 Ullswater Road, Tyldesley, Lanc, M29 7AQ. Tel: 0942 873473.
My local contact is ————————————————————

Child Poverty Action Group, 1 Macklin St, London WC2B 5NH. Tel: 01 405 5942 (2–5.30pm Monday to Friday).

Cleft Lip and Palate Association, 1 Eastwood Gardens, Kenton, Newcastle Upon Tyne. Tel: 0912 859396.
My local contact is ————————————————————

Compassionate Friends, 5 Lower Clifton Hill, Clifton, Bristol BS8 1BT. Tel: 0272 292778. For bereaved parents.

Cystic Fibrosis Research Trust, 5 Blyth Road, Bromley, Kent BR1 3RS. Tel: 01 464 7211.

Down's Syndrome Association, 4 Oxford St, London W1N 9FL. Tel: 01 580 0511.
My local contact is ————————————————————

Family Planning Association, 27–35 Mortimer St, London W1N 7RJ. Tel: 01 636 7866.

Foresight, Association for Promotion of Pre-Conceptual Care, Old Vicarage, Church Lane, Witley, Surrey, GU8 5PN.

Foundation for the Study of Infant Deaths, Fifth Floor, 4 Grosvenor Place, London SW1X 7HD. Tel: 01 235 1721/245 9421.
My local contact is ————————————————————

Gingerbread, 35 Wellington St, London WC2E 7BN. Tel: 01 240 0953. For single parents.

Haemophilia Society, PO Box 9, 16 Trinity Street, London SE1 1DE. Tel: 01 407 1010.

Health Education Council, 78 New Oxford St, London WC1A 1AH. Tel: 01 637 1881.

HIPS. Help in Plaster and Splints, 22 Claudius Gardens, Chandlers Ford, Hampshire, SO5 2NY. Tel: 042 15 68223. For parents of children with CDH.

La Leche League, BM 3424, London WC1V 6XX. Tel: 01 404 5011.
My local contact is ————————————————————

Maternity Alliance, 309 Kentish Town Road, London NW5 2TJ. Tel: 01 267 3255.
Excellent newsletter—I last paid my subscription (£5) on ——————

MENCAP. Royal Society for Mentally Handicapped Children and Adults, 123 Golden Lane, London EC1Y 0RT. Tel: 01 253 9433.

MIND. National Association for Mental Health, 22 Harley St, London W1N 2ED. Tel: 01 637 0741.

Miscarriage Association, 18 Stoneybrook Close, West Bretton, Wakefield, WF4 4TT. Tel: 0924 85515. 11–1.30pm and 6–7.30pm.
My local contact is ————————————————————

Muscular Dystrophy Group of Great Britain, Nattrass House, 35 Macauley Road, London SW4 0PQ. Tel: 01 720 8055.

The National Association for Deaf-Blind and Rubella Handicapped, 311 Gray's Inn Road, London WC1X 8PT. Tel: 01 278 1000.

National Association for the Welfare of Children in Hospital, Argyle House, 29–31 Euston Road, London NW1 2SD. Tel: 01 833 2041.

The National Childbirth Trust, 9 Queensborough Terrace, London W2 3TB. Tel: 01 221 3833.

My local contact is ⸻

The National Children's Bureau, 8 Wakley St, London EC1V 7QE. Tel: 01 278 9441.

National Eczema Society, Tavistock House North, Tavistock Square, London WC1. Tel: 01 388 4097.

National Society for Phenylketonuria and Allied Disorders, 26 Towngate Grove, Mirfield, West Yorkshire. Tel: 0924 492873.

One Parent Families, 255 Kentish Town Road, London NW5 2LX. Tel: 01 267 1361.

Parents Anonymous for Parents under Stress. Tel: 01 263 8918.

Prisoners' Wives and Families Society, 254 Caledonian Road, London N1. Tel: 01 278 3981.

Royal College of Midwives, 15 Mansfield St, London WC1 0BE. Tel: 01 580 6523.

My local contact is ⸻

Sickle Cell Society, c/o Brent Community Health Council, 16 High St, Harlesden, London NW10 4LX. Tel: 01 451 3293.

Society to Support Home Confinements, Lydgate, Wolsingham, County Durham, DL13 3HA. Tel: 0388 528044.

Spastics Society, 12 Park Crescent, London W1N 4EQ. Tel: 01 636 5020.

Stillbirth and Neonatal Death Association, Argyle House, 29–31 Euston Road, London NW1 2SD. Tel: 01 833 2851.

My local contact is ⸻

Thalassaemia Society, 107 Nightingale Lane, London N8. Tel: 01 348 0437.

Women's Aid Federation, 52–54 Featherstone St, London EC1. Tel: 01 251 6429. Or 374 Gray's Inn Road, London WC1. Tel: 01 837 9316.

Many of these organisations are run on a shoestring, so if you write please enclose a stamped addressed envelope.

Index